BREAKING THRU

THE BARS

Identical Twins, Identical Crime, Identical Time

by
Alisha Readus & Marisa Readus

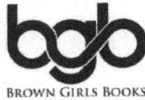

bgb
BROWN GIRLS BOOKS

Houston, Texas * Washington, D.C. * Raleigh/Durham, NC

Breaking Through the Bars © 2015 by Marisa and Alisha Readus

Brown Girls Publishing, LLC
www.browngirlspublishing.com

ISBN: 9781625176080 (Digital)
9781944359232 (Print)

First Brown Girls Publishing LLC trade printing
Manufactured and Printed in the United States of America

BREAKING THOUGH THE BARS

ACKNOWLEDGEMENTS

We would like to thank our Savior Jesus Christ for granting us the opportunity for change, and directing our paths through our journey.

We would like to thank our children for being the greatest inspiration in our lives. They have inspired us to do better, and to never give up on our dreams. They are the reason why we chose to write this book. What a wonderful blessing it is to be mothers to children who encourage us to do better and be better women for our family: Shantel, Rashard, Ramon, Asheera, Romel, Rasheed, Racheal, Roosevelt, and Reanna.

We would also like to say thank you to our mother, the late Linda Readus for praying for us when we were so lost and misled. Also, we would like to give acknowledgement to our father, the late Roosevelt Readus, who always believed in us. Although your time with us has ended, we know we were so blessed to have a mother and father who planted so many wonderful seeds in our lives. We thank you both for loving us and being strong enough to let us grow up, but kind enough to support us when we needed you. We were so blessed to have you as our parents.

We would also like to give a thank you to Lydie Barnette for being a wonderful photographer and working so well with us and our children. Her contact information: Facebook: Lydie @ Lydie Barnette or by phone at 714-235-4248 for all your photography needs.

ALISHA

CAUGHT UP IN THE RAPTURE
OF LUST & MONEY

Chapter 1

This was not the life I envisioned for myself. This was not the way I wanted to die – inside a black four-door SUV, speeding down a dark, dusty road, getting the life beaten out of me by the man who claimed to love me.

But what did I expect because there were two things DeWayne didn't play around with – his woman and his dope. And just as he'd beaten the guy two weeks ago for playing with his dope, he was giving me, his girlfriend of six months, equal time in the kick-ass department.

"Noooo, please," I screamed as DeWayne hit me in the face like I was a dude off the street. His friend, Snap was driving the truck, navigating the dark streets, acting like he didn't hear a thing. This was our normal, this was our life. I had accepted it from the day I let DeWayne lure me into his world, but I wanted better for myself, I really did. However, there's only so much a stripper can expect, right? My lifestyle came with fast money, lots of men (and yes, women) and even more danger. And DeWayne was as danger-ous as they came.

DeWayne Money "D" was known in the streets for his mon-ey, aggressive attitude, and for his way with the ladies. And I was drawn to him like a crackhead to a bag of rocks.

It's funny. As I lay in that back seat, wondering if today would be my last day on earth, my mind raced back to how this day had all begun.

The July sun was doing what it did best – heating up the streets of Huntsville, AL, and DeWayne was doing what he did best – making money in true hustler fashion. He was closing up a drug deal like he was on Wall Street trading stocks. Despite the fact that he had just did a Suge Knight on some guy that owed him money, DeWayne was conducting business like he had his PhD in pharmaceutical sales.

I'm not going to lie, I loved my lifestyle, but lately, my conscience had been a little more vocal than normal and on this particular day, I wanted to speak my piece. So I said, "Babe, it was a little foul how you beat that guy. You know you can't keep doing people like this. It will come back to haunt you."

That sent DeWayne into a relentless rage.

"Bitch, what did you say to me?" he asked, reaching into the back seat with a quickness I never saw coming.

As he reached to punch me, I kicked and punched at him, but my blows were no match, and he put a vice grip around my throat.

"Don't you ever talk to me like that!" he screamed, shaking my 150-pound frame like it was a rag doll. I couldn't reply because I was struggling to catch my breath. Not that I would've had a chance to speak anyway because DeWayne commenced to beating me worse than the guy he'd bloodied earlier in the day. He punched. He kicked. And I screamed. And cried, and cursed my conscience for not shutting the hell up.

"Help me!" I yelled to Snap as I tried to scramble away. "Please help!"

Snap just kept driving, his eyes straight ahead as if World War Three wasn't going on in the back seat.

"Pull over there," DeWayne told Snap, pointing to a park with one hand, while the other hand held my long brown hair intertwined in his fingers.

Snap pulled into a parking lot and DeWayne loosened his grip. I was debating how to make a run for it when DeWayne spotted two of his boys approaching the now-stopped vehicle.

"Man, what's up?" the guy asked, leaning in to see me crying, and bloodied up.

"Nothing," DeWayne said, flinging my head down. "'Cept this bitch finna make me kill her ass."

I know I looked a mess. I tasted the blood. I felt my eye swelling.

And yet, his friend simply said, "Yeah, these bitches ain't shit."

In my mind I was thinking, *Nigga, you ain't shit if you can sit there while a woman has just gotten beaten up.*

Everything inside me said get out and run. DeWayne was momentarily distracted, stepping out of the truck to talk to his friend.

My conscience said, run, escape, just get away. I inhaled, exhaled, weighed my options, listened to my conscience, and then told that bitch to shut the fuck up.

As I sat there in silence, my mind raced back in time, trying to replay the moments that led me to this mess. Just a few months ago my life was somewhat normal. I was an 18-year-old recent high school dropout who was just looking for a job. My employment search took me to a company called TCI, that manufactured computer equipment.

The portly, balding manager seemed interested in me, despite my lack of skills. I initially thought that he just wanted to give a girl a chance. But fifteen minutes into my interview, I saw that it wasn't my resume and job performance that he was interested in. He wanted to know my sexual skills as well. Although he was 30 years my senior, the man dressed nice and looked like he had more money than he knew what to do with. That, alone, intrigued me.

By the time the interview was over, it was time for him to take his lunch and he asked me to join him. We headed to a restaurant in uptown Huntsville, and had barely placed our order when he went in with the questions.

"So, are you single?" he said.

"No," I replied. "But I do have friends. How 'bout you? Are you married?"

He didn't miss a beat as he said, "Yes."

That caught me off guard because it was obvious he wanted to get with me. I expected him to lie simply because that's all the boys I'd interacted with in high school had done.

"Let me shoot straight," he continued, leaning in and licking his lips like he wanted to taste me right there in the corner booth, "I want you. As my employee and my lover. I'm willing to pay you more than my other employees, but I'm gonna expect something in return."

Now, I wasn't a virgin, but I wasn't a ho either. But then, I thought about all the dudes I'd gotten with for free. I thought about the four dollars in my bank account, and I thought about how attractive this man was. And before I knew it, we were in a hotel screwing like long-time lovers. When it was all over, I walked away with $500 cash, and feeling like a real true player.

That day, I learned the power of the pussy and decided that I was going to use it to my advantage. I worked at TCI, screwing my boss on a regular basis for almost six months.

One day I was driving down the street and saw a place called Exotic Measures and decided to check it out. I was ready to take my hustle to another level and thought stripping would be the perfect gig.

Exotic Measures was a popular place, but unfortunately they were not hiring because business was slow. Not to be dismayed, I hit up other strip clubs, and finally found the perfect fit at a place called Fantasy Five.

My interview was the most embarrassing thing I had experienced in my life because I had to get butt naked in front of a man that looked like a pervert from hell. It's one thing to be a pervert, and another to look like one.

"Girl, your body is the bomb," he told me, salivating as he spoke. "And those dance moves. Yep, can you start right now?"

I smiled, my confidence booming, as I told him I was ready to work right then and there.

My life was changing, and fast. I should've been a proud graduate with my friends in the class of 1995. Instead, I was now a stripper who had gone in the opposite direction my middle-class parents had planned. Not that they didn't love me. They were just tired of me and my bad decisions. And they were sick of my volatile relationships. They'd warned me, but since I didn't listen, they took the hard road and turned their backs on me.

So, now, where was I supposed to run? Who would help me? No one. Which is why I just laid there in the back seat of that SUV.

Minutes later, DeWayne was back in the SUV, ready to pick up where he left off.

"Snap, take me to this bitch's aunt's house," he said. "I'mma kill her and throw her body in front of her house." Then, he laughed, as he slapped me again for good measure. I don't know how long it took for us to get to my aunt's house. I closed my eyes and prayed for death to come quick. It didn't and the next thing I knew, I heard DeWayne say, "Get out the car."

I tried to stand, but my legs wouldn't cooperate and I tumbled to the ground. Both he and Snap just laughed. Not knowing if this was going to be my final stand, I pulled myself up anyway, preparing to die with dignity. All because I'd spoken my mind.

I knew my aunt would be shocked to see me. I hadn't been over here since I moved out my dad's house and in with DeWayne six months ago. But right now, I didn't care. I just wanted to get inside.

Before I reached the steps of my aunt's house, I fell again. This time, DeWayne stood over me. He had an evil grin as he reached behind him, and pulled out his gun from the spot where he kept it tucked in his pants. He pointed the gun directly in my face.

I closed my eyes and began reciting the Lord's Prayer – or what little I remembered of it.

Click!

I swear that silent click was the loudest thing I'd ever heard. I eased my eyes open and DeWayne was standing over me laughing like something was really funny. And then, just like that, DeWayne said, "So do you want me to take you to the hospital?"

I was shaking so bad. But I managed to say, "N-no. I just want to go to sleep."

I don't know if anyone saw us — it was late. But still, if they did in that neighborhood, no one would say anything, because nobody was dumb enough to come outside and get involved.

"A'ight. I'll talk to you later." Then, DeWayne and Snap just turned and walked away.

I was in so much pain that night that I ended up having my aunt drive me to the hospital. Needless to say, she was terrified and against my wishes, she called my father.

He arrived at the hospital, took one look at me, and vowed to kill whoever was responsible. My father was the type of man who wouldn't let much get up under his skin - unless it came down to his daughters. One time when I was seventeen and working at a restaurant, some nasty guy at work stepped out of line one to many times. I told my father and he headed straight to the my job. He didn't beat the guy, but he threatened him enough to leave him trembling.

So when I saw the rage in my father's eyes, I knew that he wanted to tear DeWayne apart. But even with all of his anger, my straight-laced father was no match for the ruthless DeWayne, so I simply said, "I don't know who did this. I was attacked coming home."

Much to my dismay, the hospital called the police (apparently, that's their policy when someone is the victim of a crime).

"Ma'am, are you sure you don't want to press charges?" the officer asked after taking the report.

"I told you, no. I just want to go home," I said, after I had a battery of x-rays and tests. I'd been poked and prodded; after the day I had, who wouldn't be ready to get some rest. Also, they'd told me I had a concussion, a broken rib and numerous other injuries. I just wanted them to give me something for the pain and send me on my way.

"She's not fooling anyone," my father said. "That boy she's seeing did this."

I sighed and vehemently shook my head. "No, he didn't."

"You know this is going to happen again," the officer said, looking at me pitifully. "Next time, you may not make it out alive."

"Thank you for your concern, but I'm good." I don't know why I refused to press charges. Well, yes I do. DeWayne was crazy and I was under his spell.

The officer had just left when the doctor made his way back inside.

"Well, good news, we can let you go home tomorrow," he said. "But you'll be in a lot of pain for the next few weeks."

Tell me something I don't know, I thought. I'd felt the knots on my head and couldn't even lay my head on the pillow because of the excruciating pain.

For the second time that day, the nurse looked at me pitifully and walked out of the room.

Chapter 2

Considering the beating that I had endured, sleep had no trouble paying me a visit. I had just dozed off when my cousin, Kim, peeked in my hospital room. She lived in Tennessee, but had been in town visiting her best friend for the past week.

"Hey, Alisha," she said.

"Hey, Kim." I should've known my aunt went right back and told everyone what had happened. "What's up?"

"That's what I'm trying to find out." She walked over and sat down next to me. "What's going on?"

Kim had always been someone I looked up to so I felt that it was okay to tell her, and considering she knew DeWayne from high school, she had a pretty good idea of what I had gone through with him.

I began to explain to her everything that had transpired that evening. Tears rolled down my cheeks as I recounted the horrible details. Kim sat without saying one word, although her eyes bore the same rage as my father's.

After I finished the whole story, Kim said, "Alisha, it's time to go. You deserve better than this. Let me move you to Tennessee with me and my husband."

At first, I protested, but she didn't let up. Finally, I agreed to think about it. And I did. Long after she left, I kept asking myself, was I really ready to leave DeWayne for good? Whatever I decided could change my entire life.

Finally, after a night filled with pain, and restless sleep, I made my decision – I was leaving. The next day, when they released me from the hospital, Kim came to the room to help me prepare to be discharged.

While we waited on the nurse to give me my discharge instructions, I said, "So Kim were you serious last night when you asked me about moving to Tennessee?"

Kim looked me in my eyes and said, "I was very serious. You are too young and beautiful to be putting up with this type of abuse."

I knew she was right. I really didn't want to leave my twin sister, who was happy in Huntsville, but I knew that I had to get out of Alabama and Tennessee was the perfect place. So Kim and I came up with a plan. I knew DeWayne usually left the house to handle his business around three. After we left the hospital, we waited until just before four, then went to the house to pack my stuff. I looked around out lavish four thousand square foot home, decorated with all the latest trendy gadgets and expensive furniture, and I almost changed my mind. DeWayne had given the material things I'd only dreamed of all my life. His dope money had given me the glamorous life and walking away wasn't easy.

But I knew I had to do it.

We'd just about finished and was loading the last of my boxes in Kim's car when DeWayne pulled up. Just my luck. Probably one of his neighborhood spies told him I was at home.

"Where the hell are you going?" he asked, barely giving the car he was in time to stop. He didn't ask how I was doing, if I was okay, nothing, except where I was going.

I took a deep breath and looked him in his eyes. "I'm leaving. I'm moving out of town because what went down yesterday was fucked up. I went to the hospital last night. The doctors said I was lucky my spleen wasn't ruptured or I didn't suffer internal damage. I didn't deserve that, and you don't deserve me." I don't know why I suddenly had courage. I think I was just fed up.

"You're not going anywhere," he had the nerve to say.

"I'm not debating this with you, DeWayne. I'm leaving."

He nodded his head like he was thinking. Then, finally, he said,

"Fine. Let's see how far you get without me. Ain't nobody gon' take care of you like I have."

I didn't say a word as I closed the trunk.

"Don't come running back to me," he continued.

Kim didn't say anything to DeWayne, she just stood there looking, probably hoping nothing popped off.

I was happy he didn't get violent; it was a sense of relief because I was determined to leave and never come back.

"Come on, Girl. Let's go, we got a long road ahead of us," Kim said as she got in on the driver's side and I slipped in next to her.

I know it's crazy, but there was a part of me that wanted DeWayne to beg me to stay, to apologize and promise that it would never happen again. But he said nothing and drove away.

My sadness seemed to dissipate the further we got away from the house. With each mile we traveled, I felt a sense of peace overcome me, and by the time we were two hours into our drive to Tennessee, I felt a new sense of freedom and joy.

Chapter 3

We finally made it to Kim's home and I got settled in Tennessee. Everything was exactly the way she said it would be. Her apartment was beautiful. It was a two bedroom and when you walked into the living room the design was contemporary and spacious. The living room furniture was showroom ready, it was the perfect apartment for newlyweds. And her patio. That was vacation-ready with a wicker patio set and oversized barbeque grill. My bedroom had a lovely day bed and dresser. There was even a computer already set up at a small desk in the corner. The setting was perfect, the bed was comfortable, and I was happy to be there. That night, I laid in the bed and started thinking about how my life would be without DeWayne in it. What had seemed like the impossible just hours ago, now seemed very doable.

The next day I began to look for a job. Even though I wasn't sure what I wanted to do, I knew I had to make some money. I'd lived off DeWayne, but I didn't believe in freeloading off family.

But there was just one problem: What was an eighteen-year-old former stripper supposed to put on her resume?

I took the first job offer I got – selling portraits inside of grocery stores. I would stand there all day offering family portraits for $50-$75. The money was okay, but it wasn't what I wanted to do. I stayed with it, though and eventually, I saved enough for a down payment on my own car. Kim took me around to several car lots. I knew that I wanted an Eclipse, and I found the perfect car, although it wasn't the brand new car I wanted, the 1992 version would foot the bill perfectly. It was exactly what I'd hoped for: rims, tint, and a bomb system in it. What 18-year-old wouldn't want that?

Plus, it was in my name. That meant it was all mine, no one could tell me to give them the keys or that I couldn't go anywhere. I was so proud of myself. I couldn't wait to tell people in Alabama what kind of car I had bought myself. And the list of people I felt compelled to tell, included DeWayne. Yes, I called him to brag and show him I could do well all by myself, and I didn't need him.

I remember the day I called him. I hadn't expected him to pick up the phone.

"Yeah, who's this?" he'd said, answering with his signature line.

"Hey, DeWayne," I said. "How you doing?"

If he was surprised to hear from me, he didn't let on. "I'm doing good, out here making this money. You know how I do," he said like I hadn't been gone out of his life for the past three months. "Oh yeah, Jay got busted."

I wanted to tell him that I didn't give two shits about Jay. But instead, I said, "Damn, that's fucked up." I was silent for a minute, then decided I didn't have time to play games. "So do you miss me?" I asked.

"Hell yeah I miss you."

His enthusiasm brought a smile to my face.

"So when you coming back home?" he continued. "You ain't got no man do you?"

"Naw, but I got a new car. And I'm doing really well," I said with confidence.

The conversation continued for another forty minutes, the majority of which DeWayne spent talking about why I should come back to him. I stood my ground that I wasn't going back.

That conversation led to more conversations. DeWayne became my outlet for some of the things I had to deal with at Kim's house – and there was a lot. When I first made it to Tennessee, things were cool, but as I became more and more independent (getting a job, saving money, and getting my first new car), Kim started tripping hard.

I will never forget the day Kim just up and started asking questions about a guy named Roger, who was her husband's friend. Roger also lived in the same apartment complex as us.

One day, out of the blue, she said, "So did you see Roger today?"

I wasn't ready for that question, but I managed to say, "What do you mean have I seen Roger today?" I could tell from the sound of her voice she wasn't talking about seeing him in passing. "Why did you ask me that?"

"Because one of the neighbors called me at work and said they saw you going up to his apartment," she replied.

I was dumbfounded. That someone would call themselves spying on me, and that my cousin would have the nerve to charge me up about it. Granted, I knew why Kim was tripping. Roger was married and she was probably concerned about me messing with a married man. But the last time I checked, I was an adult.

Needless to say, I brushed off her question like she hadn't asked me anything.

"You know he's married, right?" Kim said.

I wanted to tell her of course I knew. But he wasn't satisfied with his wife. At least that's what he'd told me. I also wanted to tell Kim, she didn't have to worry about me and Roger though, because his sex game was weak, I was just out for what he could do for me.

The argument escalated, until finally, I said, "I'm going to sleep." I didn't want to discuss it anymore, because what had been done was already done. What was she going to do, go tell his wife? No! Besides, it was none of her business.

Yet, after that conversation, things never felt quite right. Then, stuff just kept happening: my favorite outfit had gotten ruined with bleach. How the hell that happened, I would never know because they were already washed and in the dryer. Kim's energy just seemed to go onto a whole other, jacked up level. I would catch her staring at me from the corner of her eye. Then, in addition to all of that, one of my credit cards that I applied for when I first made it there, never arrived. She had me feeling all type of paranoid, because when I walked into the room her and her husband would be talking, and then they would all of a sudden stop and look at me like I'd intruded on a private conversation. The whole situation got to be too much and a call from DeWayne came when anything could have pushed me over the ledge.

"What's up, girl?" he asked after I answered the phone. Honestly I was happy to hear his voice.

"Nothing, except Kim on some other shit," I said. I sat there thinking back on the life he used to provide. I know I shouldn't have been talking to him, but it was hard to get DeWayne out of my system. Then once again, he popped the question on me.

"You ready to come home?" My brain knew that I needed to say no. But my heart wouldn't cooperate.

"Yeah, I guess." I don't know what I was thinking; I was just tired of Tennessee and the drama with Kim. It had been six months and I wanted my old life back. I had been hoping DeWayne would send me some money, but I couldn't bring myself to outright ask him.

"I know things aren't going well for you there," he said. "I can hear it in your voice," he said smugly.

I don't know why, but all my bravado and talk of being an independent woman went out the window. I missed my life with DeWayne. I missed the family things we did, even down to the time he and a friend killed a turtle to show me how they would take the shell off and cook it. Although I thought it was disgusting, he was so meticulous in trying to teach me that. I missed the good times we had. I missed going out to eat with him and seeing him sitting across the table from me. There were even times we would go visit Marisa and her family. Those moments meant a lot to me, and they were so powerful I decided to get the hell out of dodge and go back to him.

"I'll be there tomorrow."

I could feel DeWayne's smile through the phone. It was okay because I was smiling, too.

The next day, I didn't even say goodbye to Kim, just scribbled a note, packed my stuff up, took my $200 out of the bank, and headed back to Huntsville.

Chapter 4

Once I made it back to Huntsville, I moved back in with De-Wayne and fell into a natural groove. Life was better than ever. I guess the distance made us both miss each other because he was nicer than he'd ever been to me. He was caring, attentive, and he spoiled me something crazy. And his sex game was on a whole other level. He loved that I would be sexy, classy and dominating in the bedroom. I had learned that a lot of men would never admit it, but they loved a woman who would dominate without being told, or without them having to ask.

So my alter ego "Cherry" was that bitch, and I put it on him. Even before DeWayne, most of the men that paid me to sleep with them knew they would be dominated. That was one area, I never lacked in. Once I got with DeWayne, I settled down some, but before that, I was buck wild. I would chose the hardest, baddest guys; to make them weak, scream my name, and watch how much control I had over them at that time. I took pride in the fact that I wasn't some low life ho. I was a classy ho, and DeWayne loved my good girl look, plus the boss attitude "Cherry" would unleash on him once the doors were closed. Considering I didn't drink, or smoke weed that made me stand out as well. The men I fooled with appreciated the fact that they weren't sleeping with some highed up, sloppy drunk chick. They had a sober freak, who didn't mind putting it on them in a way that many women wouldn't or couldn't. Most of the men I messed with knew that I was just a natural born freak who would give head with more than just my mouth, have that hot and wet kitty cat that they loved, plus being double jointed, I could get flipped upside down, and not break a bone.

Yet, as much as everything seemed so right, it felt so wrong. I just didn't feel the same about him anymore and my change in attitude caused the old DeWayne to resurface.

"So, what the hell is your problem?" he asked me one day after he tried to snuggle up to me and I moved away from him.

"Nothing," I said. "You just all up on me. Dang, give me some space."

He stopped and stared at me, before saying, "Do you know how many bitches would kill to be up under me?"

"I, I didn't mean it like that," I said, trying to clean up my comment. But it was too late, he was pissed.

"I got all this shit I'm dealing with in the streets and I come home to yo' ass trippin' about giving me some attention?" DeWayne never had a problem with getting the ass, because I loved sex and he knew it. But attention is also something he wanted and right now, he was fed up about not getting it.

"DeWayne, don't go there. I was just sayin-"

"Nah, I heard what you were sayin'," he snapped. "And I'm sayin' this, get the fuck out!"

"Excuse me?" I said, looking at him like he couldn't be serious.

"I didn't stutter." He kicked the coffee table over and the top crashed to the floor. "I said, get the fuck out! Now!" He pushed me, causing me to topple over backwards.

"DeWayne, are you serious? What did I do? I said, I was sorry. I'm just tired."

"You tired all right. And I'm tired of your ass. Get out!"

"Fine," I said, pulling myself up and scrambling into the bedroom.

I started throwing things into my suitcase and minutes later, he appeared in the doorway. "Just so you know, when you leave, I'm shooting you in the back."

"DeWayne, I'm just doing what you told me to do. You told me to leave, so I am."

We went back and forth for twenty minutes, alternating between me apologizing, and him going off.

"You know what? I can't do this with you anymore," I said, grabbing my suitcase and heading to the bedroom door. Before I could get to the door, he reached up, grabbed my arm, pulled me back, and punched me in the face.

The punch knocked me into the wall, but I immediately gained my bearings.

"Don't ever hit me again!" I screamed. "Don't ever put your hands on me again!"

"Or what?" he yelled, as he leveled a kick in my right shin.

In what could've been a scene straight out of "What's Love Got to Do with It," I went Tina Turner on his ass. I swung on him with all my might. It caught him off guard because he stumbled backwards. I used that slip to my advantage and fought him with every piece of my soul.

We fought from the bedroom, to the hallway, to the bathroom. I kicked, punched, and fought with everything inside me. I was like a wild animal fighting to get out of captivity.

DeWayne was bleeding, I was bleeding, and still we fought.

And I was holding my own until he threw me through the folding doors in the bathroom. But before I got off the floor, I noticed a piece of wood; I guess it came from when they changed the door into folding doors during the renovation they'd started earlier this week. When I saw that stick laying there, I grabbed it and tore his ass up.

"Aaaaah!" he screamed as the stick connected with the side of his head. "Awww, Bitch, you done it now. It's obvious yo' ass wants to die!" He managed to get to the hall closet and I immediately remembered that's where he kept his guns.

I scrambled to get away, but he grabbed my leg with one hand, just as he managed to get one of the guns out of the closet with his other hand.

"DeWayne, please!" I pleaded as he pointed the gun at my head. I sobbed as he put the gun in my mouth.

"I'm going to blow your fucking brains out."

I cried as I once again prepared to die at the hands of the man I thought loved me. My body shivered and shook and then my heart temporarily stopped when he said, "Bye, Bitch" and pulled the trigger.

I heard the click, but I was still breathing, so I'd escaped death again.

"You lucky I'm out of bullets," he said, pulling himself up off me. He fell back against the bed. "Now, go fix me a sandwich. You done had me work up an appetite."

I cried as I crawled into the kitchen. I cried as I made him a sandwich and took it to him. And I cried when he took one bite of his sandwich, then said, "Take your clothes off."

I tried to get in bed first and then take my clothes off, but he said, "No, take it off right here." DeWayne made me strip in front of him, my hair and face a hot mess.

After a very awkward dance, he dismissed me. "Go to bed," he commanded.

As if I could sleep after a beating like that. I cried until I was all cried out. Like a brick slamming through a window in a riot, the revelation hit me. I was better than this, I was better than being someone's doormat in the name of money because it damn sure wasn't love. I'd let DeWayne buy my self-worth. DeWayne made sure I didn't want for a thing. There was nothing that I asked for that I couldn't get - from name brand clothes, to designer shoes. My hair and nails were done every week. DeWayne knew what would keep a woman around when there was no other reason for her to be there.

I loved to travel and if I said "I want to go to a theme park," DeWayne would show up the next day and say, "Baby, we are heading to Atlanta!"

We'd arrive to our destination and he'd have our whole day

planned. No matter what city we were in or where we were going, the hotels were breathtaking. It was the perfect life. Or so I thought.

Despite all of that, I was miserably unhappy. And I knew that as long as I stayed with DeWayne, there was not enough money or things in the world that anyone could give me to make me feel better.

I remember when I lived life in peace, when I would just enjoy life, laughing and acting silly. Now it was just constant drama. I was losing weight, and had no real interest in life because my life was not my own. It was all about what he did, what he wanted to do, and when he wanted to do it. I had no control over my life. He was controlling me through money, clothes and all the other things he was always willing to do.

I knew that I had to come up with a better game plan. I was tired of watching the street fights, watching the crack heads begging for a fix. It's the worst feeling in the world to watch the lengths the crack fiends would go to get a hit, to see what they were willing to do for it.

At first, I justified taking DeWayne's crack profits by pushing aside those images of the addicts, telling myself, 'They put themselves in this situation so it's their problem.'

But as much as I tried not to, I cared and it was tearing me up. At some point something had to change. This lifestyle was not for me. Plus, the risk wasn't worth it. Every day I was with him, I took a chance on being busted right along with him. It's funny how people think that no one knows, or is watching. That alone made me want to run in the other direction because he wasn't worth doing time for. So finally, after going back and forth with this man, I made up in my mind, I was done.

Chapter 5

Two days after my resolution to make a change, I found out I was pregnant. I'd gone to the doctor because I had been feeling sick and nauseated.

The doctor ran some tests, including a pregnancy test. Within 20 minutes, he came in and began to run down the test results.

"All of your tests were good you are not dehydrated," he began. "Your kidneys are fine but one of your tests did come back confirming that you are pregnant."

I was momentarily speechless. But then, I managed to say, "Excuse me?"

He flashed a I-don't-know-whether-to-be-happy-or-sad smile, then said, "You're with child. Congratulations."

I wanted to scream, *That's not good news!* But I was stunned into silence and just sat on the edge of his examining room bed.

What the hell was I supposed to do with a baby? I was 19 years old and finally decided that I was leaving this idiot, and now I was pregnant?

As distraught as I was, abortion was not an option (I simply couldn't see myself doing that). I knew that I didn't have a choice, I was going to have my baby and that meant I'd need to provide for it as well. And that meant, I was going to have to stay with DeWayne until I could pull it together - which lasted all of four months.

That's how long it took to see the neglect wouldn't work for me. DeWayne was no longer violent, but it was like he was no longer *anything*. He barely came home and when he did, he didn't have much to say to me. So one day when he was gone, I remember sitting on the bed in the hotel we were staying in for the night (we did periodically spent nights in hotels because they were his hideouts). I cried out to God. "If you show me how to get out this situation, I promise I will never come back again," I pleaded.

I was sure that God had simply ignored my prayer, until a few weeks later, when this girl I knew from the streets approached me as I was walking to the front door of our townhome.

"What's up, girl? What you been up to?"

"Nothing much," I said, staring at her uneasily, wondering why she was at my doorstep.

She looked over her shoulder like she was about to give me a good piece of gossip. "Girl, you know DeWayne is talking to some female."

I struggled to keep my emotions in check. "Excuse me?"

She seemed all too happy to dish the dirt. "Yes, Girl. I saw him with her last night over Boo's house."

"Oh, for real?" I calmly said. "Well, thanks for the information."

I continued into my house, not giving her the satisfaction of seeing me lose it. But I was ready to lose it. I was hanging on with DeWayne, putting up with the neglect and the beatings, and all that we'd been through, and now, he was cheating on me – and not even bothering to hide it!

For the rest of that night I waited for him to come in. How could he do this to me? If he was that unhappy why didn't he just leave me the hell alone? I paced back and forth across the room for what seemed like hours. I felt like my heart had been shattered and I didn't even have all the details. I just knew that I didn't deserve to be cheated on. Shoot, I didn't deserve anything that DeWayne put me through.

I felt a flutter in my stomach and my hand instinctively went to my stomach. "What am I going to do? How am I going to take care of this baby?" I mumbled.

It was about three in the morning when he came in the house

and I was sitting there, as if everything was okay.

"Oh, you're still up," he said when he noticed me on the sofa glaring at him. "Well, can you go to the store and get me some cereal?"

I kept my cool as I said, "Yeah, that's fine; I can do that."

He then gave me the money, went into our bedroom and in minutes, he dozed off. I was disgusted on so many levels. Not just the fact that he'd been cheating, but that after being out all night, he walked in and sent me back out to the store. Me, his pregnant girlfriend. At three in the morning.

I didn't know how I was going to take care of my baby, but watching him passed out on our bed, I knew that I was going to find a way.

I made sure he was in a deep sleep by opening the door to the bathroom and closing it several times. There was no movement from DeWayne.

After that, I started slowly getting my clothes together and putting everything into a suitcase. I probably should've left before he came in, but I wanted to look him in the eyes one last time. I needed to tell myself it was truly over.

I made sure that I had everything I needed and wanted to take with me before I left. Besides my clothes, all I had was the $60 dollars he'd given me. I wasn't sure if that would be enough to make it to Birmingham, but it really didn't matter. I was done with him, and this life he called balling. I was tired and now I knew there was another person to think about. Now that I was expecting a baby, I had to be more responsible.

I grabbed my things, slowly closed the bedroom door, and ran down the hall as fast as I could periodically looking back to see if he was behind me. Once outside, I put my things in the car, but before I got inside, I realized that I did not have the registration to my car. I tiptoed back in the house, grabbed the papers, and ran out even faster than before, but this time I was in tears.

I think I was crying because in my heart, I knew that it was really over. The lies, the danger, the lowlifes. It was over.

As I drove down the street, I remembered there was a gun in the glove compartment of my car, and I didn't want to take that with me. I had a plan, though. I had to drive out to his mom's house in the country. There were some things I needed to get from there, and I could leave DeWayne's gun with her.

It took about forty-five minutes to get to her house because she lived in the country. It was dark, because it was so early, but I knew his mom would be up. She woke up every morning at four-thirty like clockwork because she had to be to work at six-thirty. I knocked and waited for her to answer. As I stood on the other side of her door, I was debating whether I should be honest and tell her I'm leaving DeWayne.

"Who is it?" I finally heard on the other side of the door.

"It's Alisha," I replied.

Of course, she was shocked to see me. I could see it in her eyes when she opened the door.

"Hey. What's going on? Where is DeWayne?" she asked, peeking over my shoulder to see if he was in the car.

"Oh, he is in Huntsville," I said. "I just needed to drop some things off."

She studied me for a moment and I don't know if she could see the tears I was fighting off, but she said, "Alisha, what's going on?"

I looked her in the eyes and said, "I can't take anymore, I'm tired of this lifestyle, plus I found out he was cheating on me," I cried.

She didn't say a word as she stepped back for me to come in.

"I just need to get a few things," I mumbled.

She nodded, but still didn't reply.

I went into DeWayne's bedroom, which his mother still kept as some kind of shrine to her only son. I grabbed a few of my items that I had left there, slipped the gun in the dresser drawer, and then told his mother goodbye.

Once I was about twenty minutes away from her house, I

stopped and used a pay phone to call my mom. I called collect. Unlike DeWayne's mother, I knew mine would be asleep, but I also knew that she would pick up the phone. That was the one thing about my mother, she was always was right there, at the right time. She knew the life I was living was wrong, but she still prayed for me and trusted God that one day I would come home.

As soon as I heard her voice, I started sobbing. "Mommy, can I come home? I'm tired, I'm just tired!" I was crying so hard, I could barely catch my breath.

She didn't even ask any questions. She just said, "Yes, come on home. It's okay."

Her words comforted me through the phone. "I'm on my way," I finally managed to say.

"Drive safe and I will see you in a few hours," she said.

As I began to drive down the street, I knew there was another life waiting on me, another start that only God knew. I remembered the prayer I prayed a few weeks before, asking God to help me escape that lifestyle. God did exactly what I prayed for, and with each mile that I drove away, I felt free, freer than I'd felt in a long time.

By the time I made it to Birmingham, it was after nine in the morning and I knew my mom would be at work. Even though she knew I was coming home, that wasn't going to stop her from fulfilling her responsibilities. I headed straight to her school, and when I walked into her classroom, I fell right into her arms.

"Thank you, Mom," I said.

She held me as she said, "You're welcome. And everything is going to be just fine now. You're home."

After a few minutes of comforting me, my mother said, "Alisha, I have to ask you something. How did you make that collect call?"

I shrugged, even though I knew what my mother was talking about. Her phone didn't take collect calls. My mother had it set up that way because my sister and I had run up her bill in the past.

But for some reason, my call had gone through. I tried to recall if I'd done anything special. I said, "I don't know. I remembered that you didn't take collect calls, but I took a chance considering you might have changed it."

My mother smiled as she pulled me into a hug again. "Child, I haven't changed anything. That was God. He wanted you to let me know that you were coming home."

That made me smile. I believed what my mother said. God had truly looked out for me.

Chapter 6

I had been four months pregnant when I arrived in Birmingham and taking care of myself and my baby had been a huge priority. I told my mother the day after I arrived and she had stepped up to the place to be by my side throughout this pregnancy.

My mom appeared to be just as excited as me considering this was my first baby, and her second grandchild. My mom was a school teacher and loved kids so my pregnancy experience was wonderful because she was so supportive. During the time I was there she also watched as my stomach began to get bigger and bigger.

My mom and I spent a lot of time together. Our relationship grew and I gained a new respect for her that I never had as a teenager. My mom showed me once again that she was an ideal woman of God. Her heart was pure; in all that she did she had the heart of God. I should have never disrespected her as a young teenager or at any point in my life. That was one of the reasons my twin sister and I were in Huntsville in the first place. She sent us to our father when there was nothing else left for her to do. Marisa and I were seventeen when she sent us away, and on a destructive path. Our father tried to help us get it together, but I guess that growth was something that had to come in its own time.

Needless to say I was a different woman when I came back to my mother and now, she had my love and respect, as a mother and as a woman. I had grown to understand her more, which allowed me to respect all that she was and all that she was trying to do for me.

And she especially had my respect on February 16th, 1996 when I gave birth to my son, who came in weighing 8lbs 2oz. My mom was right there when I pushed him out.

When I held him, it was amazing to see and know that he had been growing inside of me, and now I had this beautiful baby looking up at me.

For months, my son and my mother were enough for me. I loved taking care of him. I loved that he depended on me. After awhile, though, I didn't want to just stay home with him. I was ready to head back into the workforce; I was ready for all that this new life had to offer me.

As happy as I was to be a mother, though, it wouldn't be long before the fast life trumped motherhood.

I returned to Huntsville, Alabama when my son, Rashard, was about two months old. This time, I didn't go back to DeWayne; I lived with my twin sister and her husband. Although I enjoyed being a mother, it didn't come as naturally as I thought it would. It was hard to get up at night for those midnight feedings and get up before the sun to feed my son.

Not only that, the street life started calling my name; I just couldn't leave that lifestyle alone. So I began to go out clubbing and hung out all times of the night. The street life, also gave me the chance to meet lots of men and I started sleeping around with many of them, once I found out they would pay for the goods. And it helped make ends meet when things got tight. Yes, I knew it was wrong, and yes, I said I would never return to that lifestyle again, but at least I wasn't back with DeWayne or in a relationship with a drug dealer. So I kept telling myself that I hadn't gone back on my promise to God.

One day, I ran into a guy that I used to go to school with and we began to talk; it was an instant attraction. Eric told me that he had recently gotten a divorce and was just chilling in an apartment that him and his homeboy had together. His apartment happened to be right up the street from where I was staying with my sister.

We started going out and six months later, I found out that I was expecting another baby. I guess I shouldn't have been surprised since I didn't always remember to take my birth control pills. I wasn't upset about the baby, though; I really liked this guy and felt that he was a genuine person. He would be a good father.

A few days after I found out, I headed over to his mom's house to share the news of my pregnancy with him. He had been living back over there with his mother since his lease was up at the apartment a few weeks before I found out I was expecting our baby He wasn't there, but his mother, who I had met a couple of times, was. So I decided to go ahead and tell her the good news.

"We're having a baby," I said right after she invited me inside.

Her lips tightened and her eyes narrowed. Definitely not the reaction I had expected.

After a couple of seconds, she said, "You know my son is still married?"

My mouth dropped open. "Hell no, I didn't know that!"

"I told Eric I don't like being in the middle of this mess," she added as she shook her head. "But you need to know this."

I was furious! Why did he feel that he had to lie? It took everything in me to stand up and walk out of the door. I was still shaking when I went outside. I left his mother's house feeling dazed and confused. I wanted to break his neck, but more than anything, I wanted to know about this wife. I wanted to know who she was, and where she lived. I felt that she needed to know who her husband had been sleeping around with, and I needed to find out where they stood in their marriage. For my baby's sake.

So over the next few days, I made it my business to ignore his ass, I was so mad and felt so deceived. The one thing I was doing was investigating, trying to dig up dirt on him so one day one of my friends informed me that she would see him over at an apartment across town late at night. I took that information and ran with it. I was going to make my presence known. I felt that if I went over there when he was at the apartment with his wife, he couldn't deny knowing me, he couldn't deny being with her, and I could bust his lying ass.

After a few days I decided to just approach her at her apartment, ready for war.

I banged on the door to her apartment. I expected some frumpy looking chick to open the door. Much to my surprise, Eric opened the door.

His eyes bucked in shock. "Alisha. . . wh-what are you doing here?"

I looked at him and said, "What are you doing here?" When he just stared at me, I added, "I just wanted to stop by and say hello." I was so calm. "Is wifey home?"

All of a sudden, a voice called out, "Who is that? Who is at the door?"

Eric tried to scoot outside, and close the door behind him. But I wasn't about to let him get off that easy.

Before he could close the door, I screamed, "It's his soon-to-be baby mama!"

Eric's hand immediately went to try and cover my mouth. I don't know if I was more hurt or angry, but the inner bitch in me was fighting to get out.

"Tell her who I am!" I screamed. "You lying dog! Tell her!"

"Girl, what's wrong with you?" he hissed, trying to push me off the porch.

"The question is what's wrong with you?" I was still screaming. I hoped the whole damn apartment complex heard me.

"You can't be coming over here acting like this," he said, his voice shaking like he was panicked.

My emotions betrayed me and tears started streaming down

my cheeks. "You told me that you got a divorce," I cried. "You told me that you weren't married anymore."

I had planned a whole, "I'm putting your ass on child support" speech. But I was so hurt that I couldn't remember all the things I'd planned to say.

"Eric, what the hell is going on?" The woman, his wife, I guess, was now standing in the door.

"Nothing. Go back inside." He tried to wave her away. "This crazy chick is trippin'."

I was already the gasoline and his comment was the match that completely set me off. I jumped on him, screaming and crying that he was going to pay for lying to me.

Needless to say, things continued to get ugly and I ended up running away from him when I heard the siren of the cop car coming. The last thing I needed was to be pregnant and in jail.

Eric didn't bother calling me anymore after that night. I was just going to have to have this baby on my own. It was hard for me to believe, because I thought Eric was such a good guy, but I was wrong about him.

Later that month, I was walking by the store when I saw him and his best friend at the store right down the street from my apartment. I paused, and looked through the window at Eric, his friend, and the two women they were with. By this time, I was very frustrated and beyond angry because in the weeks since I'd confronted him, Eric acted like nothing even happened. He acted like I wasn't expecting his baby.

As I watched the four of them inside that store, I became even more hurt. For all that I was feeling, someone had to pay. So I went into the store and the moment, Eric saw me, he stepped to me.

"Don't come in here starting no shit," he said.

As I looked at him in his face, I said, "You already started it." I pointed to my belly and his date's face followed my gesture. "I need some money for our baby,"

"Your baby?" the girl said, looking at me, then looking up at him.

I don't know what it was, that poor girl had nothing to do with anything, but her squeaky, little voice pissed me off and I went at it with her.

"Yeah, it's his baby, and?" I said, daring her to say something to me.

"Well, who are you?"

"None of your business. This is between me and Eric."

"Eric is my man," she had the nerve to tell me.

That was it. I couldn't take anymore and I shoved her so hard, she fell to the ground. Even as I stood there, looking down at her, I knew it wasn't her fault. She just was with the wrong man at the wrong damn time.

"Oh, my God," the other girl who was with her tried to come to her aide and when she pushed me, we got into an all-out brawl. It didn't matter to me that I was carrying a baby. There were hands and feet flying everywhere.

Eric tried to pull me back, but he couldn't. So, he grabbed his date and pulled her out to the parking lot as if that was going to stop me.

I followed them. I was a crazed madwoman. I don't know if it was the hormones or the hurt, but my intent was to cause havoc in Eric's life and in the life of anyone who was around him.

Even as the four of them hopped into Eric's car, I yelled and screamed. But they weren't going to get away that easily. When Eric backed out of his spot and sped off, I jumped in my car and I chased them.

I don't know what I was thinking, but I was just tired of being dogged – first by DeWayne and now, by Eric. Eric, the good guy, was acting like his child and I didn't exist.

I guess that sent me over the edge. It was like I just snapped.

That's why I kept following them, through the streets and then onto the freeway. The car chase went on for miles; they drove like they were being chased down by the police. I knew I was taking a chance of being chased by the police myself, or even having a wreck, which could hurt me and my baby. But at that point, nothing mattered. I was blinded by rage. All I wanted to do was see them hit a pole, or run off the road, anything to ease all the hurt that was raging inside of me.

Eric made a sudden turn off the freeway, swerving suddenly so that I couldn't follow. But even though I backed up, they'd disappeared, which was good for them because if I'd gotten close enough, I had every intention on rear-ending them into a ditch.

It still took a couple of days after that, but eventually, I accepted the fact that Eric was not going to be in my son's life. And I hated that I had to sink to such lows before coming to that realization.

After that, my mother suggested that I stay away from men. But considering that I did not like being single, I was always open to meeting new people. So it didn't take me long; about four months after that, I met a guy named Jonathan. I met Jonathan at the corner store. He drove into the lot so crazy while I was opening my door to get out of the car.

"What are you trying to do, kill me?" I yelled at him.

He smiled as he pulled his car to a stop and got out. "Naw, pretty lady."

I didn't know what he was smiling at. I folded my arms and glared at him. "Oh, you just like driving crazy in a parking lot for no reason, huh?"

The way he looked at me, I had to laugh and he laughed with me. And that's where our lives began - at the corner store.

We stood there and talked for a while.

The one thing that attracted me to Jonathan in that instant is that he knew how to hold a conversation. He didn't just jump right into "do you have a man" questions. He told me he was living in an apartment with a few friends and I told him that I had an apartment and a son. I didn't have to tell him that I was pregnant; he could see that since I was five months pregnant by now. That didn't seem to bother him because he said, "How about you give me your number and we get together sometime?"

Without hesitation, I gave him my number. Later that week he called me, and eventually he began to come over on a regular basis. I explained the whole spiel on how my unborn child's father and I weren't together because he lied about being married.

"That's understandable," he said. "You're not gon' have no baby daddy drama, are you?"

"No, he is completely out the picture," I replied.

Jonathan nodded his approval and once I gave him that reassurance, we fell into a natural groove.

Jonathan was laid back, he didn't club and go out all of the time. He liked to just stay home and hang out. So that made me slow down, get out the streets and focus on family.

For a while, Jonathan and I had a really good low-key time together.

Chapter 7

Before Jonathan started to come around and before things got serious between us, I used to go to church with my friend, Brittney.

Brittney was a good friend because she cared about my heart, and my relationship with God; I would go to Bible study and to church with her. It was a small church and honestly, that was what I needed – the intimacy.

The women in that church never judged me, they never said 'You shouldn't be doing this' and 'You shouldn't be doing that'. They just prayed with me, and spent time with me. They never said a word about my being pregnant and never asked me about my baby's father. I really appreciated that.

I went to church every Sunday for months, but then, eventually, Jonathan moved in with me, and once he moved in, I stopped going to church. I enjoyed spending those leisurely Sunday mornings in bed with Jonathan.

So one day when we were laying around the house, someone knocked on the door. When I answered, I saw it was the women from the church…two of them.

"Hello, Sister Alisha," one of the ladies stated.

Another lady named Sister Margaret, said, "We haven't seen you at church lately. We were concerned about you and just wanted to stop by."

Standing there, I felt so ashamed. But I lied before I knew it. "Yeah, I've stayed home because I haven't been feeling too good the last few weeks."

"Okay, we just wanted to make sure that you and Rashard are okay," Sister Margaret said.

"Yes, we are fine."

"Can we pray for you before we leave?" Sister Margaret asked.

I didn't expect her to ask me that and I wasn't sure how to handle it. It was like I'd abandoned God, but He hadn't abandoned me. He'd sent these women to my doorstep.

"Yes, I don't mind at all," I said.

The four of them gathered around me and said a quick prayer, asking God to heal me and restore my health. I kept my eyes closed as I prayed with them and I prayed that God would forgive me for lying.

I hugged each of the women before they left and promised that I would see them soon. When I returned to the bedroom, Jonathan looked at me.

"Who was that?" he asked.

"Just some ladies from this church I used to go to." This was the first time I was talking to him about church. I'd shared everything with Jonathan, but I don't know why I hadn't felt comfortable enough to share my spiritual side with him.

He didn't say anything about it and I didn't mention church again. Of course, I didn't go back like I promised those women.

There were so many things going on in our life. Eventually, Jonathan and I began to talk about moving to Birmingham because nothing was popping off in Huntsville anymore. And it wasn't just that way for us. My twin sister was talking about leaving her husband and so moving to Alabama would be a great opportunity for her, too.

We started thinking about Alabama because Jonathan had a friend that he had introduced me to named Tamiko. He knew Tamiko because her sister had a baby by his brother. Tamiko told us that she was moving to Birmingham because she heard they had a lot of work there and that's what we were looking for, too.

The only problem was, Jonathan could not stand my twin sister; he felt that she took advantage of me all the time, he felt she tried to run my life. Once when we were together she expected me to drop everything for her, despite the fact that I had other plans with him. She wanted me to kick him to the curb because she didn't like him. She had done this on various occasions before Johnathan came in the picture. He was the first one to point it out, saying, "Your sister thinks she runs you." I looked up to my sister and I never thought of it that way, but I started feeling like some of the things he was saying were true. In the end, though, they learned to get along for my sake. He tolerated her because of me, but I hoped that if we all moved to Birmingham together, the move would be good for all of us. I was hoping that it would bring unity and she would see what I saw in him just enough to stop dogging him so bad. So we all decided to move to Birmingham.

I talked to my mother and she agreed Marisa and I could come home. She was happy to have us back, but there was one thing I had to make sure she knew.

"Jonathan is coming. So he needs to stay with you, too," I told her.

"Absolutely not!" she replied without hesitation.

I rolled my eyes when I heard my mother say that, knowing, I would've never done that if she could see me. I should've known my ultra-religious mother wasn't about to condone her daughter living with her boyfriend. Not under her roof.

She and my father had divorced when my sister and I were seven, and she hadn't had another man under her roof since then because she wanted to respect us and keep us safe.

So, I told Jonathan to stay in Huntsville until I could get my own place and then me, Marisa, and my son moved to Birmingham.

Marisa found a job right away, but considering my baby was almost due, there was no way I could start working. My mother was okay with that, though. She just wanted me to deliver a healthy baby.

A few weeks after I moved to Birmingham, the day came when the doctors decided to induce labor. I didn't want to go through it alone, and even though the baby wasn't his child, I called Jonathan and asked him to come to Birmingham. He'd gone through the pregnancy with me, so he agreed.

On June 4th, 1998 my twin sister and I went to the hospital and they hooked me up to the IV to start the process. I was in labor all day and as each hour passed, the pain worsened. I didn't want an epidural because it was against what I felt a woman should do. The way I looked at it, what if there was no medication to help me during my labor? Then I wouldn't have a choice; I'd have to go through it naturally. And considering I had previous back surgery at seventeen, a needle going in my back was not one of those things I thought was smart to do.

So I gave birth to my son naturally at approximately 12:49 a.m. It was amazing how fast he came – once he decided to come. I'd been there all day and the nurse had just told Johnathan and Marisa it was okay if they left and changed places with my mom because I was only about four or five centimeters dilated.

"It's going to be several more hours," the nurse said. "So, it's okay if you want to go home and get some rest."

But almost as soon as everyone walked out of that room, I screamed to the nurse, "I need to push!"

She was unfazed. "You probably just need to use the bathroom," she replied.

I wanted to scream that I knew the difference between having to go to the bathroom and having to push a human out of my cooch.

At that moment, I knew more than the nurse because my second son was born just a few minutes later. And my whole family (and Jonathan) completely missed the birth.

A few days later, I took my son to my mother's house and we all settled in there. But after a few weeks, that restlessness started setting in again.

Even my mother could feel it. She started getting frustrated with Marisa and I being there because we had begun to be rebellious. She would tell us to clean up or be home at a certain time and we wouldn't. Considering I had just given birth to my second son, there was not much I could do, but Marisa was making it hard for me, because as long as she continued to act out of line, we both might as well have been.

But my attitude wasn't the best either. I walked around like my mom owed me something and I could do whatever I wanted. Eventually, that became too much for my mother and she insisted that we move out as soon as possible.

Considering that only one month before, I had just had the baby, I did not have the means to move out, nor was I physically ready to move out and I certainly wasn't ready to start working.

One day, my sister and I had been out and about and we both made it home to find a set of scrubs, a small television, panties, and kids clothes. I was so upset and I did not know what to do. Instantly homeless and nowhere to go, I had no job I felt so lost.

Marisa immediately got angry. "She got some nerve! How could she just put all our shit outside?"

I was dumbfounded. I knew we had been trying my mom — leaving the kids with her, keeping the house a mess, and not following her rules and coming home any time that we wanted to. But I had no idea she was fed up enough to really kick us out.

"Someone must have told her to do this," I said, "because mom has never been so heartless."

Before I could say another word, Marisa kicked the front door in. "Fuck this!"

That night we tried to grab as much as we could because honestly we were breaking an entering. So if she rolled up and we were in her house she would probably call the police or maybe the guilt is what we both were trying to avoid. Suddenly I remembered that my mom was at our grandparent's 50th anniversary, but she would be home soon. With the amount of frustration and anger I had toward our mom, I can honestly say I wanted to tear that house into pieces. But really, who could blame her for throwing us out?

But even though I understood my mother, I was still pissed. Marisa and I grabbed our clothes, shoes and jewelry. But we didn't stop there. We even took a TV. Then, we took our belongings and found a motel.

When we got her on the phone, she said, "I'm tired of you; you're both disrespectful, and need to take some responsibility for your lives."

"You were still wrong for putting us out," I told her. At that moment, all I could think about was how wrong she was for throwing us out, considering my son was one month old at the time. I thought she would at least insist that my kids stay. But she mumbled something about me "taking care of my responsibilities."

So now that I wasn't going to live with my mother, that meant I had to start working with being four weeks postpartum. I knew that could be dangerous, but I did what I had to do. Marisa and I watched each other kids. One night I would work and the next night Marisa would work, just so we could pay for the motel.

Eventually, after two weeks, the motel money ran out, and we moved into a shelter. But we had no intentions of staying there, so we worked our tails off as C.N.A. at nursing homes, and hospital through a temporary agency that paid daily until we got into a place to live. Marisa was approved for a house to rent and once again Jonathan came down. But this time, since we weren't with my mother, he stayed. So now, Marisa, Jonathan, and I, and soon after, Marisa's boyfriend, Mark, were all living in the same house with our children. It was a house full of adults and things were about to get bad, real quick.

Everyone in the house was irresponsible. We were all working, we all had money, and we had divided up the bills. But no one wanted to take responsibility and the bills didn't get paid. For me, Jonathan was the worst because I expected so much from him. But he was selfish;; he just wouldn't pay any bills and on top of that, he couldn't see where he went wrong in the entire equation of our financial distress.

Because of that, Jonathan and I argued all the time and it turned out living with him in Alabama wasn't good for me. He was mean when he drank and we argued, saying things that hurt me and destroyed my self-esteem. He drank a lot, to the point of passing out on several occasions. Mark and Jonathan had no problem getting high on weed and drinking together. The thing that was crazy about that, though was that they didn't like each other for one reason or another.

But overall, Jonathan was just unhappy and he made everyone suffer because of that. He treated my sons as though they were only there for him to fuss at. I couldn't totally blame him for that; he hadn't been around kids, so he did not know how to build relationships with them. He only did what he knew, and that was fuss about everything that went wrong.

There were times he wanted me to neglect my children, not pay attention to them or even leave them home alone just so he could have what he wanted. Many times, I went along with him, knowing it was wrong. But what I also knew in my heart was that this was not what I wanted for my life.

Chapter 8

Everyone was having a hard time, but Jonathan still withheld money, he still wouldn't help pay any of the bills and he even stole some of my money. I will never forget one particular day, when he went to Huntsville to visit his family and friends. I was cool with that because they were in his life before me and I respected his relationship with all of them. But the one thing he failed to do was respect the fact that I was his woman.

The entire time he was gone, I had this gut feeling that he was going to cheat on me. Considering I am second to no woman, there was no way in hell I was about to allow this man to run out on me and think he could come back with his germs, kissing all on me. So the entire time he was there, I kept calling and kept calling. When I called over to his sister's house, she just said, "Oh, Jonathan just left. Him and his brother went over to Kevin's house."

I didn't act a fool, but I still couldn't shake that eerie feeling in my gut. I was sure that he was cheating.

So once Jonathan made it back to Birmingham, and he played that 'I missed you, baby' game on me, I didn't feel that it was sincere. But since I didn't have any proof, I let it go.

The next morning when he asked me to get his jacket out of the car, I jumped at the chance.

Once I got to the car, I turned into Inspector Gadget, searching everywhere. It wasn't long before I saw a number written on a napkin.

I didn't tell Jonathan I found it. I didn't say anything; I just tucked it away. Later that night when I got to work, I called the number. And sure enough, a woman answered.

"Who is this?" I demanded to know.

"This is Trina, who wants to know?" she asked like she was used to women calling and charging her up.

Trina! I instantly recognized that name as one of Jonathan's ex-girlfriends.

I didn't waste any time. "Did you and Jonathan fuck?" I asked point-blank.

She had the nerve to laugh.

"I will come right up there and kick your ass if you don't tell me what the hell happened."

Considering that Huntsville wasn't too far away I was about to leave work and go make good on my threat.

Finally, she said, "Look, don't call me with this mess. I saw Jonathan at the store. We had planned to meet up at a hotel, but I didn't show up because someone told me he had a girlfriend. So the way I see it, you need to be thanking me for having someone respect your relationship because it's obvious your man doesn't."

I didn't totally trust her word, but I trusted my gut feeling, and it told me everything she'd said was the truth.

I hung up and geared myself up, so that once I got home, I was gonna act a special kind of crazy. I walked that house, I threw the napkin with the number on it at him as he got ready for work.

"I talked to your bitch," I said without even saying hello. I didn't even care that we weren't alone. "She told me everything."

He looked startled. "What are you talking about?"

I looked down at the napkin and he knelt down and picked it up. His eyes widened when he read the number.

"Umm-hmm," I said, watching his reaction. "She told me y'all were supposed to meet up at a hotel."

"I didn't fuck her," was all he said as he crumbled up the napkin.

"But you wanted to," I snapped.

I could tell he was about to give me some lame lie, so I just yelled, "Get your shit and get the hell out of this house!"

"Why? I told you nothing happened!"

It wasn't my plan, but we went back and forth, arguing until finally, I guess he decided to leave. But on his way out the door, he snatched some of my money from the dresser drawer.

"You better not take my money," I screamed.

Jonathan ran toward the front door, and I was afraid he was gonna get away. Until out of nowhere, Marisa grabbed a big knife from the kitchen and ran after him.

"What the hell?" Jonathan yelled when Marisa caught up to him.

It all happened so fast. The two of them struggled back and forth until Marisa swung the knife. He jerked away, and the entire left sleeve of his jacket was ripped off from her grabbing him. He swung around, knocking her to the ground and then, he managed to get away – with my money.

"Marisa!" I screamed as I ran to her side. I was so afraid. My sister was pregnant and she'd already had a scare, thinking she was having a miscarriage.

I got my sister up from the floor and made her go into her bedroom to lay down.

"What are you gonna do?" she asked me.

I didn't know. I had no idea where Jonathan was going. I didn't know if he was going to come back or bring me back my money.

Later that day, after I made sure Marisa was okay, Jonathan called and said, "I didn't want you to fuck my shit up, Alisha. All I was trying to do is protect what's mine."

"That money is mine and I want it back!"

He told me that he would. I didn't really believe him, but later that day, he brought me back all of my money and got the rest of his stuff and moved out.

We separated, but over the next month, we worked things out and eventually started anew.

Chapter 9

Our financial situation caught up with us a couple of months later, and our landlord served us with an eviction notice.

We did our best to draw out the eviction process. But things were bad and getting worse and we all had to do something quick.

In the midst of desperation, you can find yourself doing things you wouldn't normally do. I was trying to live right and my heart was in the right place, but I was influenced by my sister and began to think the same as her.

My sister had been living on the other side for a while - hustling men for money, checks, and only God knows what else she was doing in those streets, but somehow she kept money in her pocket. I didn't judge her though, because I knew she was only doing those things to help pay the bills.

Considering Marisa didn't get caught the last time when she got money the illegal way, I thought that I wouldn't get caught either.

Marisa and Tamiko were able to get away with over $15,000 dollars. It was a bank scheme: Marisa deposited a check that was made out to her from a company that had several million dollars in their account. No one with that much money would miss such a small amount as $15,000. It had worked the last time, surely it would work this time.

Even though the walls were drawing in on us quick, I wasn't sure that I really wanted to do this. But something needed to change, something needed to happen.

Jonathan and Mark were no help; they were just as clueless as we were and offered no encouraging words nor any solutions to help change our situation. We were the blind leading the blind, needing to make something happen. If only we would have known what waited ahead for us and for our future, we might have made a different decision.

Right around this time, Sam, Marisa's boyfriend's brother started talking about a scam to make some money.

"We can open up bank accounts," Sam said. Then, he went on to explain how he would get accounts in elderly and disabled people's names. Sam would use all their personal information to start the account and they'd be none the wiser.

Without hearing all the details, Marisa instantly wanted in. Sam was hesitant because Marisa was pregnant, but she insisted on joining the scheme.

"I don't care," Marisa told him. "I can do this, I *have* to do this to pay some of these bills and do a lot of other stuff for my family."

Just the thought of her having a chance on a come up made her eyes twinkle with dollar signs.

My conscience had gotten the better of me and I opted not to take part in the scheme, even though Sam had it all worked out. He had connects at major businesses (many of whom operated with million dollar budgets) and his people were going to draw up fake checks only for deposit purposes. It was going to be Marisa's job to take the checks to the bank and deposit them. Then, a few days later, after the checks cleared, she'd go withdraw the money.

Sounds easy, right? That's what I thought, especially when I watched my sister work with Sam and then successfully pocket thousands and thousands of dollars.

Even though I was envious of the money, I didn't want to get money that way and I tried to appeal to my sister, telling her how wrong what she was doing was.

But Marisa didn't want to hear it. "I don't want to be a hypocrite like all of those other so-called Christians," she told me one day after I'd tried to explain that religion and relationship were two different things. "I have to fix some things about me first anyway," she added. "Besides, I'm getting serious cash." She waved a stack of hundreds in my face and my heart sank into my gut. Not only because she wasn't listening, but because I found myself wanting a piece of that pie, too.

It was hard for me to resist, especially since I was new in my walk with Christ. I would see my sister come home daily, with bags and bags of new clothes. She'd go out to eat, party all the time, and spent money like crazy on whatever she wanted to. Meanwhile, I sat at home struggling, trying my best to make ends meet.

Day after day I watched my sister thrive in her illicit lifestyle and soon, my mind was thinking of all the things I could do with that money if I had it. I could buy things my children needed, a much needed new car, and so much more.

I knew that Marisa had no direction because she was selfish, self-centered, and buck wild, but at least she was happy. And I was not. I was trying to be faithful to God and with my financial situation, each day seemed harder than the last.

Jonathan wasn't helping either. He still wasn't being responsible with money, but every time I even mentioned what Marisa was doing, he shook his head.

"Don't do it," he warned. "Don't get involved in that mess."

"Do you have any better ideas?"

He shrugged. "I'm just telling you what I know. Don't be messing with banks; that's a federal crime."

For once, Jonathan made sense, but he still didn't have any solutions for me.

So, all I could do was watch my sister and I began to be sucked into the window of deception that my sister was stuck in. I began to want to keep up with the Joneses and to have as much as everyone else. I was honestly tired of doing the right thing and living the right way because it was so hard.

I continued to go to church, trying to fight the demon that was leading me the wrong way, but it wasn't working. I did not get what I wanted and needed fast enough. What I needed was strength; I needed courage to stand against Satan. I needed God to intervene, but He gives us choices, and ultimately, I made the wrong one.

I really did try to fight it, though and one day as I was sitting on the bed in my room, contemplating committing the crime. I suddenly heard a voice say, *"Seek ye first the kingdom of God and all His righteousness and all these things shall be added unto you."*

It was clear that God was speaking to me. I felt in my heart, and in my soul. I wasn't sure what it meant, but I knew it was God talking to me, letting me know that I was not alone and he was with me.

Right then, I made up in my mind that I was going to stand with God no matter what, even with all of the temptation all around me.

I was still in a relationship with Jonathan, and I tried not to look at what Marisa was doing; I tried to focus on just Jonathan and my children. But things didn't change much with him. In fact, our situation got worse. When I left to go to church, Jonathan would accuse me of going to meet other men. He made it seem that my motives were not because I was seeking God, but seeking the man of God for my life.

I was so unsure on what to do with Jonathan, and how to handle our relationship. Then, throw in my financial situation, and I finally went to my sister. I was ready.

"I want in," I told her.

She looked at me with apprehension all across her face. "Are you sure?"

"Seek Ye First The Kingdom Of God And All These Things Shall Be Added To You."

I pushed aside the voice in my head. I'd been seeking some relief and I wasn't getting anything in return. I was tired of being poor. I was sick of barely having anything. I was so ready to get out of this situation that we were in. So I just said, "Absolutely." Then, I smiled as I thought about all that I was going to do with the money I was about to make.

Chapter 10

Marisa and I headed over to Sam's house. I had visions of my new life, with plenty of money, dancing in my head. We made it to our destination and Sam seemed happy to have me on board. He jumped right in, telling me again how the scam worked.

"So, you're going to take these checks to the bank." He handed me a stack of what seemed like twenty checks. "You'll deposit them into the account. Go through the drive-thru, not inside. Pull up to the window and ask for a deposit slip, fill it out, and give it to the teller. That's it. Go to another bank and do the same thing. We don't want to put all the checks in the same bank. We'll wait three days for the checks to clear, then you'll go to another branch of that bank and withdraw the money."

I nodded. Now what was so hard about that?

The next day, dressed in street clothes, my sister, our kids, and I piled into our car to head to the first bank to make our first deposit. I was nervous as all get out as we pulled up to the drive-thru window. I filled out the deposit slip and waited with baited breath. The clerk's voice came through the speaker.

"Will there be anything else for you today?"

I finally breathed. "No, ma'am. Thank you."

My sister gave me an 'I told you it was easy look,' and I pulled off and headed to the second bank.

I was still nervous, but not as much as before as I pushed the Call button.

"Yes, I would like a deposit slip," I told the bank teller. She sent me one, I filled it out, then returned it with the checks.

A few minutes passed, then she said, "I'm sorry, I will need your driver's license to complete the transaction."

My heart started racing. *My driver's license? For what?*

My gut told me to speed off at that very moment, but all I could think about was I'd be leaving all my money behind, when I probably was just overreacting.

But the look on my sister's face scared me. "That lady doesn't need your ID," Marissa hissed.

"But she asked for it. What the hell am I suppose to do?" I whispered back.

"Ma'am, did you hear me," the teller continued. "I need your ID."

I had to think fast. "Oh, I'm just making the deposit for a friend who owns the company."

"I understand, but I still need your ID in order to process the deposit."

At that moment I noticed the camera at the corner of the drive-thru pointed directly at me. I let out a heavy sigh and handed her my wallet.

"What are you doing?" Marisa snapped.

I motioned for my sister to be quiet as I sent my license inside. "Here you go, ma'am."

Marisa leaned back in the seat and began furiously shaking her head like that was the dumbest thing I could've ever done.

And when the teller said, "I'm sorry, you'll have to come inside to complete the transaction," my gut once again told me that my sister was right.

Even still, I parked my car and went inside.

Marisa just continued sitting in the passenger seat, shaking her head.

"Just watch the kids, I'll be right back."

Inside, the teller greeted me with a smile.

"Thank you, Mrs. Allen," she said, referring to me by the name written on the check. "I'm so sorry for the inconvenience, but checks of this amount have to be processed inside. You can have a seat at my desk and I'll be right with you."

I did as she instructed as she went to the back. She returned just a few minutes later and slid behind her desk. "We're almost done," she said with a smile. "How are you today?"

I nodded, still nervous. "Okay."

Her warm smile put me at ease. "It's my first day back at work. I'm struggling because my nineteen-year-old daughter died two weeks ago."

As a mother, my heart immediately went out to her. "Oh, no. I'm so sorry."

We talked for a minute about her daughter and were only interrupted when I heard Marisa's voice.

"Alisha, we need to go. The kids are getting impatient." At the time Marisa's oldest daughter Shantel was only three, Rashard was two, and Ramon was eight months old. It is very hard to entertain children in that age range especially while sitting in a car so I really needed to speed things along without becoming suspicious. So I stated

"Marisa We are still waiting on the deposit to clear," I told her. "This lady was just telling me her daughter died recently."

Marisa gave me the biggest *And?* look and I tried to motion for her to chill.

The woman's phone rang. She picked it up, listened as the person on the other line said something, and then replied, "So, the checks have cleared?"

Now, that made me really nervous. We didn't need the checks to clear because we were only making a deposit. Suddenly, I thought, Marisa was right. It was time to get the hell out.

"I'm going to go check on my kids," I told the teller. "I'll be right back."

She didn't say a word as Marisa and I darted to the door. We had just opened it when we came face to face with two uniformed police officers.

Chapter 11

"Seek ye first the kingdom of God and all His righteousness and all these things shall be added unto you."

The voice that I'd pushed back earlier, once again roared loudly. But judging from the way the officers were glaring at me, it was too late.

"I'm sure you know why we're here," the first officer, a short, pot-bellied man said.

Of course, neither Marisa nor I were admitting to anything.

"No," I said, while my sister remained quiet. "But I need to go check on our kids." I tried to step around the officer. I didn't think it would work, but it was worth a shot.

"No, ma'am," the officer said. "Step back inside. We'll take care of your kids."

He motioned toward another officer that had appeared behind him. The officer turned around and left the building. By this point, people were staring at us. The warm smile that had been on the bank teller's face was replaced with a look of disdain, and I would have given anything just to turn back the hands of time.

The teller turned and led the way to the back of the bank. I assumed we were supposed to follow, so I did. No one said a word as they sat us down in a large conference room. I wanted to cry when the door opened and our children walked in, looking shocked and scared. Had we known that we would have been arrested there is no way we would have taken our children with us. They were so young, my son Rashard was only three years old, Ramon was eight months. Marisa's daughter was four years old, and she was pregnant, so this was a big hot mess that we got ourselves and our children into.

We both sat looking around the room at our children, who had no idea what was going on, so they just sat. All I could do was pray and ask God for forgiveness.

But in my heart I truly believed I was not going to prison. *God knows my heart.* That's what I kept telling myself. But no sooner had that thought entered my mind, I remembered that I hadn't listened to God. Still, I knew He was faithful, and gave grace and mercy. So I was hoping He was about to bestow all of that grace upon me.

The door swung open and more police officers entered. There were so many you would have thought we'd robbed the bank at gunpoint.

The first officer who had stopped us, sat down in front of us. Without any fanfare, he cut straight to business. "You ladies will be going to jail today so you need someone to get your children."

My body weakened. I slid down in the chair and let out a slow wail.

"Is there someone you can call?" the officer asked.

I was too busy sobbing, so my sister said, "Our mother."

That elicited an even bigger cry from me. Our mother was as a teacher and this meant that she'd have to leave school. And not only that, but her car was not working properly; we'd been taking her to work, so now she would have to find someone to bring her up there to get the kids.

What could we tell our mother? What would she say? These weren't the daughters she had raised. This was going to kill her.

The man slid a phone in our direction. Knowing we didn't have a choice, Marisa slowly picked up the phone. She glanced over at me and all I could do was give the look of how I was feeling and that was completely distraught. She dialed the number and put the phone to her ear.

After a few seconds, she said, "Hey, Ma, Alisha and I need your help. We got into some trouble."

I could only imagine what our mother was saying.

Marisa paused. "I know, Ma. We'll explain everything, It's bad and the police are here. Can you just get someone to bring you here to pick up the kids?"

I couldn't make out what my mother was saying, but I could hear her voice and I could definitely tell that she was screaming. That only made me moan louder.

After Marisa hung up, the officers gathered up our kids.

"Mom?" my oldest cried.

My voice shook as I said, "It's okay, baby. Just go with the policeman. Granny is on the way."

All three of our kids started crying as the officer led them out. The other officer got up and followed him.

Once we were alone, I managed to suck up my tears enough to go off on my sister. "I am not about to go down for this by myself; I am going to tell on Sam." My mind had already been churning. These people had to know I was at the bottom of the totem pole. Surely, they'd want the guy at the top and I was more than willing to give him to them.

Marisa looked at me, horrified. "You can't tell on Mark's brother!" she exclaimed. "I live with Mark, he'll make my life a living hell."

I wanted to tell my sister that if I didn't give up Sam, she didn't have to worry about her life because her life would be spent behind bars!

Marisa and I went back and forth, until finally, she agreed with me. We *had* to give up Sam. Marisa was four months pregnant, she couldn't go to jail. And I couldn't leave my kids either. This was surely a bad situation for the both of us.

The door opened up again and instead of the uniformed police officers, two men wearing black suits entered. They all had guns and badges on their hips.

"We're with the Secret Service," the taller of the two men said.

Marisa and I exchanged glances. I knew we were thinking the same thing. This was worse than we could've possibly imagined.

Chapter 12

While we were rattled, the agents were calm and cool. Two of them slid into the chairs directly across from us.

"You know this is pretty bad?" the tall one asked.

We both nodded.

As if in sync, the second one picked up the conversation. "But we know you two are not the master minds behind this."

That was my cue. I scooted to the edge of my seat, prepared to go full Aretha Franklin on them and sing from the rooftops.

"No, we sure aren't," I said. "And I will tell you everything you want to know. I'll even take you to his house."

The tall agent released a small smile, but the other agent had his eyes fixed on Marisa, who was shifting uncomfortably.

They immediately started in with the questions.

"So which one of you ladies opened this account?" one of them said.

I replied, "Sir, we didn't open this account and we don't know who did. We were only supposed to make the deposit."

Marisa sat staring at me, I can only imagine what was running through her mind, but I wasn't going down for this.

The other agent asked, "I'm going to ask you again. What's his name?"

"Sam" I replied, this time with no hesitation.

The officers exchanged glances, then said, "We'll be back."

They left the room. Marisa was so pissed, she wouldn't even look my way.

After a few minutes, the door opened again and the first uniformed officer re-entered. "Your mother is here to get the kids.

She can take your car, if you agree to let us search it."

I didn't have the slightest clue about my legal rights, but Marisa, on the other hand, wasn't trying to cooperate.

The way I was thinking, I was in enough trouble and I wasn't giving the Secret Service any more reasons to make life hard for us, so I simply said, "Yes, you can search!"

Marisa rolled her eyes at me. I guess because we both knew there was enough evidence in that car to send us directly to jail. But the way I saw it, they were going to search regardless, so we might as well let them, then maybe they'd tell the judge we'd been cooperative.

The knots in my stomach did a slow dance while we waited in the small room with the agents. Marisa didn't say a word to me, and that was okay. I was trying to figure out how to get out of this.

When the police walked in fifteen minutes later, whispered something to the agent in charge, then handed him a stack of the checks, I knew there would be no get out of jail card today.

We had $260-thousand worth of checks in the car. A federal crime had no doubt been committed and these cops weren't going to cut us any kind of break.

"Take 'em in," the lead agent said.

I started sobbing again. I guess the agent felt some type of sympathy toward us because he said, "Cuff them outside so their kids don't have to see them like that."

That eased up some of my crying, but couldn't stop the pain inside my stomach. Our mom was standing there, looking really disappointed as she took custody of the kids from the police officers. My mother used to always lecture me about how my decisions not only affected my life, but affected everyone that was in my life. I never really gave any credence to what she was talking about – until now.

Once we were taken outside, Marisa and I were both read our rights, and then handcuffed. They separated us and took us to jail in separate cars.

Riding in the back of that police car was the lowest I'd ever felt. Even when DeWayne was beating me, even with all the jacked up relationships I'd been in, at least I had some control over those situations. I was the one who'd made the stupid decision to stay.

But now, I had no control. I couldn't decide anything.

Inside the police station, Marisa and I were united again.

"What are y'all doing here?" one of the female guards asked when they took us over to the area for processing. "You know better. Y'all are too pretty for this."

Considering I felt very ugly that day, I didn't believe anything she said, except the fact that we had no business in that jail.

It was one of the most downgrading experiences either one of us had ever had. We were stripped searched, told to bend over and cough. We had to shake out our hair, open our mouths, lift up our arms and breasts.

I'd always heard what people went through being arrested, but this was ridiculous and embarrassing. I felt stinky and nasty after what seemed forever, which only was actually a 15 minute drive, we finally arrived to the county jail.,

Once booked, we were put into separate rooms to be interrogated. I didn't know why, but I thought we'd be sent to a cell, where I had planned to just cry myself to sleep. But the federal agents that were at the bank reappeared and began drilling us; well, I should say they were drilling me because I don't know what was going on with Marisa. But I assumed she was experiencing what I was.

There were questions upon questions, and I knew that everything I said, they'd used against us. Periodically, the agents would switch out to go and ask Marisa the exact same question that they had just asked me.

I was sure that it wasn't as hard on me as it was on Marisa because I was willing to tell it all, so with every question, I gave them an honest answer. I felt that lying at this point would only hurt the situation. I didn't have a single thing to lose.

Once they were done with their questioning, the lead federal agent said, "Well, I got good news and bad news." I held my breath as I waited for him to continue. "You can go home tonight without bail, but you have to sign a waiver agreeing to come back and meet with the Secret Service agents tomorrow."

I wanted to shout for joy.

After they explained everything to me, I was sent to a holding cell until Marisa was done, and then we could call our mom to come get us.

Marisa came into the cell not to far after me, but again, she didn't say anything. That was okay because as I sat in the jail cell, all I could think about was my children. I sat there praying and promising God that I would be the best mother ever if He got me out of this predicament.

An hour later, my mom arrived with my kids in tow.

Marisa was silent when we stepped into the lobby and saw our mother. But I said, "Mom, I'm so sorry."

She didn't say a word. She didn't have to, though. I saw the hurt and disappointment in her eyes. And I felt so bad about it. As we headed home, complete silence filled the car.

My mother didn't even say anything once we dropped her off at home. I think her silence hurt more than any lecture.

At home, Jonathan met me at the door. "What happened? Where have you been?"

"We got caught and were arrested," I whispered. I kept my voice low because I didn't want my kids being any more traumatized than they already were.

Jonathan's mouth dropped open in shock. "I told you this was a bad idea!"

I glared at him as I walked holding the baby, and telling Rashard "come on its time for bed." Once they were settled I walked back into the living room and Jonathan began pacing across the living room. "Oh my, God, they gon' be watching all of our asses now!" he yelled. "You don't ever listen! I told you not to do it, but you did it anyway."

I didn't even know what to say at this point to defend myself because for once, he was right. But my silence didn't deter him. He kept on and we ended up arguing all night.

Exactly what I *didn't* need. I was already under the bus, and he kicked me even further under.

Chapter 13

As promised, Marisa and I showed up to the Secret Service office the next morning. They led us to a small bare room with nothing but an old wooden table and six chairs surrounding it. The only other piece of furniture in there was one of those old metal TV stands, with a 36-inch TV and VCR sitting on it.

We had barely sat down when the agents went straight in on Marisa.

"You've been a very busy lady," one of them sneered.

I looked at my sister in confusion as one of the officers pressed play on the VCR. A grainy image of my sister, wearing oversized sunglasses appeared. She was at a teller's station. That was no surprise to me; I knew she'd been doing this con with Sam for a couple of months, but only smaller levels. But then, the video cut to another video of Marisa at another bank, another shot at another bank, and another, and another.

"What the hell?" I muttered. Like I said, at first, it was no surprise, but the way my sister's clothes changed in the videos, it looked like she'd been doing this for months and months and months – way before Sam came and talked to us about this.

Marisa, once again, didn't say a word. She just sat there looking stupid and saying nothing, so the agent turned to me.

"Do you know anything about this?" he asked.

"No!" I exclaimed. "I had no clue about any of this." I knew Marisa had started having large amounts of money, but I wasn't sure exactly where it was coming from. And I didn't really ask because I knew what kind of life my sister was living.

"So, you want us to believe that your sister was bringing in all this cash and you had no idea where it was coming from?"

Marisa finally spoke up. "I did explain it to her one time, but I played it down and she just shook her head and said she didn't want to get involved."

Marisa was right about that. I knew about that one time. That one time with the fifteen thousand dollars.

The agents asked more questions, and Marisa finally started answering with no problem.

When they asked her about Tamiko, Marisa said, "I haven't spoken to her in months. I have no idea where she is."

Once they finished questioning Marisa, they slid a picture across the table and in our direction. I hadn't needed to snitch on Sam, because they had a big 5x7 photo of him.

"Do you know him?"

Without hesitation, I said, "Yes." I'm glad I did speak up because that picture was followed by a slew of others. They had pictures of everyone, people we knew, and other people we didn't know.

By the time they finished with us, I was not only exhausted and fearful of what lay ahead, but I was also downright pissed off at my sister. The whole reason we'd been caught was because they had been on the lookout for my sister. They had been looking for her because of all that she'd been doing with Tamiko!

A week later, we weren't the only ones in trouble behind this check scam. The Feds caught up with Sam.

About one month after this all began, Marisa and I were sub-poenaed to go to court. We arrived to our arraignment. During this time the charges were ran down I was being charged with Attempt To Defraud the bank and Conspiracy. Considering that Marisa had two felonies she was charged with Bank Fraud, Attempt to

Defraud The Bank, and Conspiracy. During this time, we also received a court-appointed lawyer. Immediately, we knew that we needed to find a private attorney if we wanted to stay out of jail. There was just one problem. We were broke.

We started calling around anyway. One lawyer told us he would not touch the case unless we paid six-thousand dollars upfront. Another said, he'd need his money put in escrow, and yet another said we could be looking at a final bill of more than fifty-grand. We didn't have a choice. We'd have to take the court-appointed lawyer.

The man who was appointed at the arraignment was very nice, but not so positive.

"Are you going to plead guilty or not guilty?" he asked.

We both agreed to plead guilty because there would be no use in a fight when we knew that what we did was wrong.

"Okay," he said. "Then I'm just gonna shoot straight." He paused and looked at both of us. "You're looking at a minimum of one-to-five years in prison."

That was something that I really didn't want to hear, considering that I was convinced there was no way I could be sentenced to any time. I hadn't received one brown penny. Then throw in the fact that this was my first crime; I truly believed that it was possible for me to bypass such a harsh punishment or any punishment at all.

Of course, that wasn't the case. The prosecutor had no mercy on either one of us and wanted us both taken into custody that day.

Fortunately, the judge did not agree to do that with us, although Sam was taken into custody right away. It turned out that our judge had previously sentenced Sam to prison and explicitly told him that if she saw him again, he would get hard time.

Marisa and I were allowed to remain free until we would pled guilty or not guilty but I couldn't stop wondering why I was being punished so harshly.

Like I said, this was my first conviction and I was on the lower end of the deal, so why would I get prison time? Marisa figured she was getting what she deserved because she had two felonies and had ill-intent when committing the crime.

While we were waiting to for court , the Secret Service continued to ask questions about the person who opened the accounts, but we truly did not know. We didn't know if it was Sam, we didn't know who it was. But despite how hard I tried to comply and co-operate with the Feds, the stress still weighed heavy on my heart, with frustration and even anger. Nothing seemed to be going right.

Things continued to get worse and worse. I felt nothing but completely hopelessness.

Chapter 14

The entire process was draining, and since we were already in a bad spot financially, we ended up getting evicted from our home while we waited. Marisa and Mark found an apartment, and Jonathan and I broke up and went our separate ways. But I couldn't find anything; it was hard without money. But I didn't have any options. Things were so bad between me and Jonathan that even though he got an apartment, he would not allow me and my children and to stay with him. And I couldn't stay with Marisa because Mark had decided that he wanted for them to live alone. So I was left homeless.

I slept, with my kids, in abandoned homes, then, we would go to soup kitchens in the daytime to eat.

We did this night after night, and one night I had no place to go because I and Johnathan had broken up, so, I went over to Marisa's house.

My sons and I stood outside on her porch knocking until she answered. "Can me and my kids please come and sleep here for the night because I have no place to go?" I asked my twin sister.

She had the door only cracked halfway open. "No," was all she said.

"Please, just let us sleep on the floor," I begged. "We will leave in the morning."

She remained adamant and shook her head. "No. Mark doesn't want anyone living with us. I told you that." Then, she shut the door.

I felt so lost, so hurt, so abandoned by everyone I loved.

But the one thing I kept consistent was attending church . Despite what I was going through, I continued to seek God. He was the only thing I had to hold onto doing this time.

The day after my sister turned me away, I went to the church and talked to Cedric one of the assistant pastors . Once I explained to him that I'd been sleeping in my car and abandoned houses, he spoke to a woman who attended the church as well, and she stepped in to help. She offered to get a hotel for me and my children for three nights.

I was so grateful. It was only three nights, but that was three nights that I didn't have to worry about my kids. Once we made it in the hotel, she fed us, then left us alone.

As my kids slept, I prayed, thanking God for touching that woman's heart to bless us with a place to stay.

As I prayed, I felt a peace come over me and I muttered, "God, I trust you. Even when the three days are up, God I trust you to be the keeper of me and my two children."

I dozed off and was later awakened by a noise. It wasn't loud, but it was loud enough to wake me up; it was a kind of gurgling

As I looked around the room to make sure my children were okay, I saw my son, RaShard, on the floor shaking. Because I had worked as a nurse, I knew immediately that he was having a grand mal seizure, considering I had several years of working in the medical field it was without a doubt he was having a seizure. I immediately called 911, I also called Cedric, the assistant pastor from the church, and began to explain to him what was happening I explained

"Rashard is having a seizure!" I yelled. "Meet me at Children's hospital!"

As I waited on the paramedics, his shaking got worse. I screamed his name.

"RaShard! Oh, my God, baby, mama's here!"

My other son, Ramon, sat on the bed, trembling also, but I know his shaking came from fear.

Suddenly, he stopped shaking and I felt a flicker of relief – until I realized that he wasn't breathing anymore. I screamed as loud as I could, calling his name and calling on God. Right before the ambulance arrived, my baby took a small breath.

When the paramedics came into the room, I told them, "He took a small breath but he's still not responding to my voice."

His eyes were glossy, his body was totally limp, looking lifeless.

"What hospital do you want to go to?" the paramedics asked as they went to work on him.

I gave them the name of the hospital, grabbed my other child, than raced behind them out the door. I followed the ambulance in my car, trying desperately not to have a panic attack.

All I could see was my lifeless three-year-old son's arms fall to the side. I burst into tears as I made a quick left off the freeway. I needed to drop Ramon off with my sister so that at the hospital, I could focus on RaShard.

When Marisa answered the door, I was so distraught.

"RaShard is on his way to the hospital! Can you watch Ramon?"

My sister didn't ask any questions as she raced to the back of her house. I stepped inside, but waited right at the front. I could hear her talking to Mark, and then, she rushed back to where I was standing.

"Mark will watch him. Let's go."

The last time I'd seen her, she was turning me and my sons away. But when it came to emergencies, we were still family. I let my sister take control as we headed toward the hospital. It seemed like one of the longest rides of my life.

As Marisa drove, I sat on the passenger side praying for my son and asking God to spare his life. Then, after a few minutes, God gave me a peace in my heart. An unquestionable peace in my heart that no matter what, my son would be healed. I will never forget how God showed me that RaShard was going to be okay.

Once we arrived at the hospital, some of the church members

had already made it there; I guess Cedric made quite a few calls because the pastor and Cedric arrived at the same time. It was amazing already to see how God was moving on the heart of the people in my life.

A nurse took us right back to check on RaShard and words can't express what I saw when I got to the center of the Emergency Room.

RaShard ran toward me screaming, "Mama!"

My mouth dropped right along with many tears. I picked him up and hugged him so tight. I was in complete disbelief. It was a true miracle to see him awake, moving around, and moving around so soon.

There were two things that I would always remember about that night: how lifeless RaShard was when the ambulance took him away, and then how God told me he was going to fine.

Later that night, the doctors did advise me to get RaShard further testing and an MRI to see if there was anything abnormal in his blood work or neurological system. I agreed to take him to see a neurologist as soon as I could.

It didn't matter that things weren't going well in my life. I was going to make sure that my son was well.

I contacted the doctor they referred me to for his testing, and she took us right away. She was very detailed and did all of the testing that was needed to prepare ReShard for the MRI as well as other tests that would support anything that they may find in the MRI. One of the tests that had to be completed for RaShard was for Muscular Dystrophy. That was scary, but I wanted my son to be tested for everything so that we could take care of anything the doctors and the tests found. Plus, my faith was strong – God had already told me that everything would be all right.

Due to his age, when it was time for his surgery just days after he'd had the seizure, they had to sedate RaShard to complete the MRI, which would take up to an hour.

As my mom and I sat there in the waiting room, the doctor

entered.

"We got back some of RaShard's test results and there were several that came back abnormal," she said. The look in her eyes told me that the prognosis would not be good. "Ms. Readus, I regret to inform you that your son's test for Muscular Dystrophy came back positive."

It felt like someone had taken a sledgehammer and slammed it into my stomach. The doctor continued talking, but much of what she said was a blur. Well, with the exception of the part where she informed me that my son would be unable to walk by the time he turned ten.

While she was still talking, I immediately began to pray for my son and I did not question God's ability to heal him. Although I stood on faith, my heart felt heavy and sad for my son. Feeling unsure of what he would have to go through with this new disease, it made me re-think the future I had for my own life.

Chapter 15

It felt like so much was going wrong in my life; everything seemed to be failing, and falling to pieces. At the time, I was still homeless, lost, and didn't know what to do. As I shared with several church members what my children were going through (now with this disease) someone told me about a woman named Melva, who, after hearing about my situation, wanted to meet me.

I was hesitant at first I thought to myself, *Why would she want to help me?* But despite what my fear, I decided I had no room to complain or doubt and agreed to meet her. We sat up a time later that day so she could meet my children and I. We went to meet her and within minutes, she opened her home to me and my family.

Melva began to tell me "God told me that you could stay in my home for three months and after that, you would have to leave," she said.

I was in shock. This woman didn't know me, yet, but yet she really wanted to help me not because she had to but because she wanted to.

My smile was full of gratitude. I didn't mind at all that she'd given me a timetable because I was grateful for her just allowing us to have a place to stay.

My sons and I moved in with Melva and within days, I was able to find a job as a Pharmacy Tech. I found a daycare center where I left my sons while I went to work every day.

When I got paid my first check, I couldn't wait to give Melva something. But she would not allow me to pay her anything.

"This is my work for God, no charge," she told me.

Again, I was in awe of her and of what God was doing.

Melva was more than just a place for me to stay. She was such an encouragement and placed a lot of wisdom inside of me spiritually. We would spend time together and watch different ministries on television. She talked with me, answered my questions, and soon, I began to change. I couldn't help but change. I genuinely wanted better for my life.

My son's life had been spared. My life had been spared and now, I wanted a better life altogether. I wanted a better career, to be a better mother, and even to value myself more.

For the first time in my life, I saw myself as a respectable woman instead of a sex object. In fact, it was during that time that I made up in my mind that I would not have sex again until I was married, or at least I would try.

The time with Melva wasn't all easy, though. I bought an old car, but it wasn't very dependable. It kept breaking down, but I needed it to get to work. But then, work became challenging. I had to often call in sick because RaShard would be too sick for me to take him to daycare. I hated missing so many days, but my child was my number one priority.

Within the second month of working, though, I was fired for calling in sick too much. That made me sad, but I didn't know what else I could do. I had to take care of my child.

Eventually, the three months deadline arrived and my time was up at Melva's home. Between my car breaking down, the expense of daycare, me losing my job, my financial situation hadn't improved much in the three months.

But I had changed. I was spiritually stronger and wiser. After I left Melva's home, I went and stayed in a homeless shelter for a short time and then because I didn't have anything else to do and I wanted better for my sons, I moved back in with Jonathan.

Chapter 16

While I was trying to get my life together, our court case rolled on. Marisa and I went back to court to plead guilty to the charges we were facing.

Midway through her ramblings, the judge stopped and stared at Marisa.

"Are you pregnant?"

Marisa nodded. "Yes, ma'am."

"When is the baby due?"

"August 16th," she replied.

The Judge shook her head, then said, "Sentencing is set for September 16, 1999."

We waited for that date to arrive with great anticipation. Jonathan and I worked it out and he let me move back in. While I was there we had some great make-up sex, one of his best qualities. Hours and hours of straight getting it in his sex game was on point and he always knew that when he was with me one thing he wouldn't lack was sex, and good head. Doing the day stayed there with my sons, while he worked full time from six in the morning until four in the afternoon.

He often reminded me that he was the only one working and encouraged me to get a job, but limited transportation how could I work, plus daycare cost, it was almost impossible to do both.

"You're just living off of me," he said.

Of course, that was true, but considering that I knew my sentencing would be coming up, I didn't really know what to do in the meantime. So I did absolutely nothing, except embrace my children and the time I had with them.

A joyful moment arrived when Marisa finally gave birth to her baby Asheera on August 12th. She was so beautiful and so small. Our hearts were filled with joy, but also with sadness because our fate was still dangling in the distance among a million questions of the future, and what it held for us and our children.

Finally, September 16th arrived. It was time to face the music and find out the answer to the lingering question: How long?

On that morning I got myself dolled up I put on a pair of black dress pants, with a nice maroon colored dress-shirt with my make-up flawless to hide the fear that ran through my shaking bones. I got in the car and headed over to get Marisa. By that time Marisa had broken up with Mark, and she, ended up in a shelter. Once I had arrived at the shelter, Marisa came out looking beautiful in her red suit. We both looked like we were going on a TV or Radio interview but instead we were going to have our world taken from us. It was no bittersweet moment to this situation. It was just bitter. During the ride over, there weren't many words exchanged, we were losing our minds with fear of the unknown. While we were on our way to court, we had to drop Marisa's children off with Mark at his mother's house. I had already left my children with Johnathan so he actually was doing something worth doing, and that was watching my children while I went to court.

But once we parked and it was just the two of us, Marisa asked, "You ready?" as we stood outside the courthouse confused and scared ass hell.

Before I answered, I looked my sister up and down. She had on a red suit jacket, matching skirt and white shirt. I wore a pair of black dress pants and a button down dress shirt. We looked beautiful, but felt horrible.

I nodded, and she took my hand. As we walked into the courtroom, we saw our family; my mom, grandfather, and all of Sam's family sitting on the first row. That was one time I did not want to see them, any of them. Sam's family was there as well since he was being sentenced at the same time.

It was just terrible and very embarrassing to have to be sentenced in front of people who expected you to fail from childhood. It was like they were there to say, 'I told you so.'

We were so nervous because in court things could go favorably or just unfair and wrong. We had no control over any of it. There was so much fear and tension in the room; I could feel it. Hearts were racing and tears were flowing. Everyone waited to find out our destiny.

Marisa and I stood there emotionally prepared to meet our fate.

"All rise," the bailiff announced as the judge entered.

We did as he said, then sat once the judge gave us permission.

My sister was called up first.

"Marisa Readus, you have pled guilty to the charges before you. Is there anything you'd like to say?"

I expected Marisa to be defiant, or not say anything at all. My heart sank when she began to cry.

"I am so sorry for what I did," she sobbed. "Just please have mercy on me. I just had a baby and can't bear the thought of being away from her."

The judge looked unmoved as my sister continued to plead for mercy. Once Marisa was finished, she stepped back and stood next to our attorney.

Silence filled the room as the judge looked over some papers.

Finally, she said, "Marisa Readus, I hereby sentence you to twelve months in prison, to be followed by five years probation."

Marisa's cries became even louder and she became weaker at every word the judge spoke. This was a Federal crime, so there would be no early release. My sister would have to serve her whole sentence and miss her daughter's first year of life.

"Marisa, I implore you to take this time to find out what you want for your life," the judge continued.

"Yes, ma'am," was all my sister was able to mutter.

I was next and like, my sister, when I stepped forward, I immediately began to cry. My mind went back to the fact that I hadn't received a dime. Surely, I would not get prison time. Worst case, I wanted probation. I was praying for probation.

In what sounded like a recording from just a few minutes before, the judge said, "Alisha Readus, I hereby sentence you to twelve months in prison, to be followed by three years probation."

I stood facing her in shock as she continued talking. Finally, I turned to my attorney.

"Why?" was all I could say.

He motioned for me to be quiet as the judge shot me a look of admonishment. As she continued to explain everything to me, I stood there with a stare of disbelief. The sentence was harsh in my eyes and if my attorney wasn't going to say anything, I would.

"But your honor. . ." She needed to understand that I'd never received any money.

"Counselor, would you advise your client not to address me?"

"But, I don't understand why I'm getting the same sentence!" I rushed the words out.

The judge glared at me. "You don't appear remorseful at all," she said.

"Huh?" Where in the world was she getting that from? "I am very remorseful! I just - "

"Be quiet!" the judge yelled.

My attorney squeezed my arm trying to silence me.

"Does the prosecution have anything you'd like to add?" the judge asked.

Just as he did on the day of arraignment, the prosecutor stood. He waved a stack of papers. "Your Honor, these are the girl's school records. These twins were violent and got into constant fights while they were in school. We consider them a threat to society and have wanted to detain them since the first day charges were brought."

I turned and glared at him. I wanted to punch him in the face, but the reality of what he was saying hit me harder than any punch

I could've thrown or any punch that he could have thrown at me. I was where I was today by my own doing. It was my fault and I was suffering the consequences of my decisions.

Although I still felt my sentence was unjust, one thing was for sure - I knew there was nothing I could do to change the judge's mind. Although the prosecution made the request for us to be detained on that day, the Judge set the date for me to surrender on October 25th, 1999. On the day of sentencing, the judge asked Marisa when did she want to turn herself in because she had just had a baby. She decided on February of 2000 so that she could spend time with her new baby. A week later, Marisa decided it was best if she got her time over with and changed it to the date I was to surrender to prison. The worst feeling in the world is looking at your life and knowing that in just a little over a month, you would be in prison.

The time came for Sam to be sentenced and the judge had no mercy on him either. He was sentenced to over 47 months in prison.

Everyone in the courtroom was saddened by what had happened on this day. This would definitely be a day I would not forget.

I had so many questions:

What will happen to our children?

Would we have to fight in jail?

Would someone try to make me their girlfriend?

All of those questions ran through my mind as I stood in the courtroom. I was scared to death, and didn't know what to expect. In that moment, I even contemplated suicide because death seemed to be the better option.

Once I left the courthouse, I went home to tell Jonathan what happened. For the first time, he showed deep concern for someone other than himself. He held me and told me, "We'll get through this."

Even though Jonathan tried to comfort me, I fell into a pit of depression . . . and then it wasn't long before Jonathan returned to his old selfish ways. He would do things like bring food home, but nothing for me and the kids. His drinking got worse and he made snide comments about what was he "supposed to do" while I was in prison.

Everything seemed to be going bad for me, and just when I thought life couldn't get any worse – it did.

Chapter 17

About three weeks before I was to report to prison, I found out that I was pregnant with my third child.

That day started out like all the others, with me dragging and moping around, but this time, I felt like it was more than just the depression. I felt physically ill.

I was beyond fatigued, exhausted really and I couldn't eat. It became so bad, that I drove myself to the emergency room, where after several tests, the doctors said those dreaded words: "You're pregnant."

I burst out crying right there in the ER. Jonathan and I had been dating for over two years and I hadn't gotten pregnant before. Why now? Why now right before I had to go to prison?

"God, is this a cruel joke?" I yelled to the skies.

Right there in the hospital, I cried harder. I was going to have a baby in prison!

What was going to happen to my unborn child?

Will my baby go to the state?

Will I be able to get him back?

What was I going to do now?

Once again, a thousand questions ran through my mind.

When I finally got myself together and made my way home, I shared the news with Jonathan. He shocked me because he was so excited. That was the only glimmer of happiness – the enthusiasm he displayed.

For a few days, I felt better. At least my child had a father who was happy about him or her. But the baby wasn't enough to keep Jonathan from doing some jacked up stuff.

Like the day I glanced outside when I heard a car pull up into the parking lot. Jonathan was on the passenger side of a car, driven by one of his female co-workers. I watched him getting out the car, laughing and giggling, holding a bag of food in his hands; he was having a great time.

When he walked inside, then tossed the Popeye's box in the trash can, I went off.

"Are you for real?"

"What?" he asked, looking at me like I was crazy.

"Not only do you roll up here with another woman, but you come with just enough food for you. Me and the kids ate green beans today because that's all that's here to eat! And not only that, Ramon has been wearing the same diaper all day because he's out of diapers!"

"Look, don't start with me," he said.

I ignored his words. "How can you work every day, but we have no food, and Ramon has no diapers?"

Jonathan rolled his eyes. "I can only do so much. I'm already taking care of everything."

We argued some more and then right in the middle of one of my sentences, it dawned on me – I was repeating the same old bad habits.

When I was working I made sure everyone ate and had what they needed unlike his selfish ass. I made sure everyone was taken care of, I paid all the bills, even though Jonathan was working, too.

But Jonathan would never be that kind of man. He was just not ready for a family and no amount of me trying to make him ready was going to change that. He would always be selfish, he would always feel like his money was just his money.

He cut through my thoughts with, "If you don't like the way I do things, you can always leave."

I hadn't been listening to what he said, but those words came across loud and clear.

"You know, what, you're right," I screamed. "Go to hell. I'm out."

It was after nine, but my kids were still up, probably because they were starving. I stomped into their room, grabbed what I could in five minutes, put my son in the stroller, and took the other by his hand and then, we headed down the hill to try to seek help.

As I was walking on the dark highway, the stroller started wobbling and then one of the wheels broke off. I looked at my sons and just burst into tears. Once again, I felt completely hopeless and angry at life, but what could I do? I refused to go back.

So I kept on. I pushed the lopsided stroller with one hand and held RaShard with my other. And we walked and walked. For three miles. Once I made it to the corner store, I used a payphone and called 9-1-1.

"I was just kicked out of my apartment by my boyfriend," I said, explaining my situation to the operator. "And my two kids and I, we don't have anywhere to stay. I don't have a car, I don't have anything."

"Hold on, ma'am," the woman said. "I'm sending a police car."

As I sat waiting, I saw Jonathan drive by on the highway. I stooped down so he wouldn't see me at that store. As he drove past, I guessed that he was going to the store right next to the one where I'd stopped. He probably thought that I'd gone there because the store next door had more light and it was the store I usually went to. But after Jonathan finished his search and left, shortly after, the officer arrived.

"Are you all right?" the officer asked.

I nodded, barely able to form words through my tears. "My kids and I are just so hungry. A…and my baby needs diapers." I was shaking and so sad that I had disappointed my children and myself so much. I felt like a complete failure.

"Come on, you don't need to be out here," the officer replied. He scooped my son up out of the stroller, then motioned for me and my other child to get in the back.

"I don't have a car seat, but hold on to your son until I can get you to safety."

I was shivering as he drove off. First, he ran into WalMart and got a car seat, then he took us to McDonald's where we all ravaged the food like it was our first meal in days. (Actually, it was since we'd been surviving off green beans for a week.) Afterward, he took us to a domestic violence shelter.

Once I made it to the shelter, I had the opportunity to rest well that night. When morning came, I went into the kitchen and met several other women who lived there as well. They introduced themselves, but I remained silent. Considering that I only had about a week left before I went to prison, I had no desire in knowing about anyone else's problems or situations. I also didn't like the way the women were talking. They made it seem like they were there for a free ride, not as a safe haven that this shelter was meant to be.

This was not a place that I wanted to be with my children. And What made it worse was that I had such a short time to make things right with them before departing.

I stayed at the shelter for four days. By the time I left, I only had three days before it was time to report to Marianna, FL to begin serving my prison time. And I still had no idea what I was going to do with my children. My mother had made it clear that she was tired of me and my sister spiraling-out-of-control ways. She'd washed her hands of us, and in my mind, that meant my children as well. In reference to my father I knew that he was strong figure in my life, a wonderful father but keeping my children while I went to prison was a hell no. So I didn't even bother ask or let him know that no one else was willing to get them. I can only imagine what he would have said to me, so to avoid another disappointment, I held it in and never told him what might have become of my children while I was in prison. We truly had no place left to turn.

Chapter 18

Most of my family knew that I was heading to prison, but my relatives were the 'you-made-your-bed-so-now-lay-in-it' type, so no one had stepped in to offer to care for my children while I was away.

Eventually, right before I had to leave, one aunt stepped in and saved the day. She had always been the aunt who took care of everybody, and her love and love for Christ allowed her to open her home and her heart to my youngest son, Ramon. She would never know how much I truly appreciated her for taking him.

Once she stepped up, so did my mother, who agreed to take my oldest. I believe my mother had always planned to take my children, but she wanted me to "stew in my mess" for a while. Of course, it helped that RaShard had been approved for disability payments because of his Muscular Dystrophy, which allowed my mother to have some income while I was away.

I hated that I couldn't give my aunt any money, but she was understanding regardless.

The morning came when it was time to drop Ramon off. That had to be the hardest day of my life. I held my sons tightly in the back seat of the car, rocking back and forth as my mom drove us the one hundred miles to Huntsville where my aunt lived.

Once we arrived at my aunt's house, my heart sank, like I had just taken a ten foot dip on a roller coaster. I was getting closer to saying goodbye.

My aunt greeted us at the door. "Hey, Ramon," she sang. He giggled when he saw her. She had a way of putting everyone at ease.

I was able to spend a little more time with Ramon while Marisa and my mom got in the car and went to drop off Marisa's daughter, Shantel, who was going to stay with her paternal grandmother who lived in Huntsville as well.

My aunt and I talked and laughed, but behind my laughter was doubt and fear. I sat on the couch and would lost myself in thoughts of 'what if's' about my son.

What if he doesn't remember me?

What if I die in prison?

What if he doesn't remember how much I love him?

What if I lose custody of him while I'm away?

When my mother returned and it was time for me to leave, I walked out the door trying my best to hold back the tears. I knew Ramon wouldn't understand why Mommy was crying; I'd tried to explain it all to him, but he couldn't understand why I was leaving not to return for a whole year. He just didn't get it. Still, I didn't want his last thoughts of me to be tears flowing down my face. So I held all of my emotions back until I got in the car, and then I burst into tears.

"Why was I so stupid?" I cried. "Why was I so money hungry that I just didn't work harder to get what I needed instead of breaking the law?"

My mother looked at me, but answered with silence. My sister sat in the back seat, probably silently wondering the same thing that I'd just asked myself.

On the way back to Birmingham, we had to drop Marisa's youngest daughter, Asheera, off at her grandmother's house. While she was there, my mom wanted to have her car cleaned, so my mom, Rashard, and I went to the car wash.

I'd gotten into the back seat with RaShard, just wanting to be as close to him as I could be for as long as I could. My eyes were on my son when a song came on the radio -- T.D. Jakes *This Storm is your Test.*

"When you don't know what to do and you're going through a test you

say, 'Lord where are you?'" T.D. Jakes began speaking before the song played. I closed my eyes and listened to the lyrics.

"Lord, I'm hurting. I never thought I'd have to go through anything like this. . . it's just a storm."

Wow! At that very moment I knew that God was speaking to me. I knew that God was going to walk with me through my entire journey. My burdens that I carried for all of those months were lifted with those simple words. Because God came and directly told me this was only a test and I was going to pass.

The tears flowed from my eyes again, but I felt hope and comfort this time.

Through the rearview mirror, I looked at my mom and said, "He got me, Mommy, God got me. He hasn't left me, and He is with me."

I could see the shock on her face as she looked at me and listened to the song; she knew it, too.

We finished cleaning her car and then headed to get my sister. From there, we returned to Birmingham. We were going to our mom's house where our father would meet us to take us to Marianna, Florida.

As we rode back, not many words were needed, because there was a peace I never experienced in my life all over me. This was a journey I was about to start, but not without the hand of God guiding me through. You see, if you remember, before I did this crime that put me in this position, I had been seeking God. And I continued to see God despite that fact that I'd fallen. I didn't let my crimes nor my sins stop me from seeking the God that I knew would be with me. It was funny, though, that the God I was searching for and the answers that I'd been seeking all of that time came in the words of a song.

Needless to say we made it back to my mother's home and all that was left was waiting for our dad and saying goodbye to RaShard. As hard as the other goodbyes had been, I knew this would be the toughest. RaShard loved me beyond words, and I was unsure of how I would look him in his eyes and say goodbye to him.

But then, our dad arrived. He'd agreed to take this trip with us despite of his disappointment in what we'd done..

It was the moment of truth as I looked in my son's eyes and told him, "Mommy will back soon."

"Okay," he said.

I hugged him for about five minutes, not wanting to let go, but finally, I had too. Tears rolled down my cheeks, and he looked up at me as if he knew that I would not be coming back any time soon.

I stood and hugged my mother. "Thank you for watching my son, Mom. I really appreciate you so much for taking him in when you really don't have to."

I would never forget that moment because my mother stood right there next to my dad. And when I looked in his eyes and saw so much hurt, so much disappointment, I wanted to cry. Hurt and disappointment was all I could see on both of their faces. And there were questions on their faces, too. Questions like: How did two successful parents, who loved their children and who were always there for them, get to this point? Why did they have to face something like this?

I wanted to tell them that it wasn't their fault. We were the ones who messed up, they hadn't done anything wrong. But through all of their questions, their thoughts and their emotions, I didn't say anything.

Marisa and I finally got into the car with our dad, and headed toward the highway for the four-hour drive that would lead us to face our fate. The only good thing about this trip was that it gave us a chance to spend quality time with our father.

The best thing about our father he was always respectful, and he believed in us. He was a role model worth looking up too. We never saw our father hit a woman or disrespect a woman in any way. Our dad always took care of us and helped raise us despite our parents being divorced. He never stopped being a dad even in the midst of his disappointment.

As upstanding as our father was, our mother was, too. She never disrespected her home or allowed a man to disrespect her. She lived a good, clean life, as a woman of God. She was a role model as well. So there was no reason for us to be in this position, considering how our parents raised us. Like I said before, this was all of our fault.

We had just started the trip, when our father said, "It would be different if we were taking this trip because you were going to college, but prison is the last place I thought that I would be taking y'all."

We sat quietly with no response; what could we say? Eventually the thick air cleared and the rest of the ride was enjoyable. One thing I couldn't stop thinking about though was that I'd be separated from Marisa for an extended period of time. Because we were identical twins, we had to be separated because we were a security risk to the prison system. So while I would be staying in Marianna, Florida, Marisa would be further down in Coleman, Florida. These were the closest prisons since there were no federal prisons for women in Alabama.

The four hour journey gave us a lot of time to digest, accept, and more than anything, forgive ourselves. The fact was, we'd messed up big time, and disappointed everyone in our life.

I thought back on the people we knew who had been to prison and everyone we knew never progressed. They never did much after they were released and many times, they even ended up back in jail. Would our life be nothing but a sad song of what things use to be? Would recovery even be an option for us? That was my prayer. For both me and my sister, I prayed for the best.

Chapter 19

The Florida sun was just peeking out as we arrived in Marinna. Any other time, I imagine this would've been a beautiful scene. But today, even with the shining sun, it just seemed gloomy.

But I wasn't as sad as I thought I would be. Maybe it was because of the time we spent in the car with our father. But I was ready to get my sentence started so that I could get it over with. Naturally, I was nervous and scared, but I knew this was something that had to be done.

My dad and sister got out and came in with me and we were escorted into the prison and I was checked in by the officers there. We'd made sure that the only things I brought with me were my IDs, and my social security cards since I knew they'd be taking everything away from me.

After being checked in, the warden met with us.

"Any questions?" she asked after explaining the basic rules to me, my dad, and my sister..

"Yes," I said, raising my hand. "I'm pregnant, so what does that mean?"

"You will be treated like any other prisoner," the warden replied. "However, we do have a program set up for pregnant women. It's called the MINT Program and is designed to let the mother spend time with her baby and give you time to recover from childbirth."

That news was a breath of fresh air. That was my only question, but my father had more questions, which the warden answered willingly.

After our conversation, my sister and dad got ready to leave and head toward Coleman. With tears in my eyes, I gave both my sister and dad a hug.

"I'll see you soon and I love you," I told them, then watched them walk away.

I was still fighting my tears as the guards led me back. They took me to a nurses' station, where a nurse took blood and performed several lab tests. I was then strip-searched, while another guard packed up my belongings. After that, they gave me my prison clothes - steel-toed shoes, army fatigues socks, panties, T-shirts, and bras. All of the clothes I had on when I arrived had to be sent to my mom's address considering I didn't have anywhere else to send it to.

Once I completed all of my paperwork and found out where I was going to be sleeping, they gave me a tour of the facility, showing me where the dining hall was, the gym, the track and the place where they held GED classes. I found out I was going to be on the second floor.

All of the officers seemed to be nice, but I honestly wasn't buying any of it. I didn't trust anyone. All of those stories I heard about prison, I wasn't about to trust anybody; I just wanted to get in and get out.

By the end of that first day, I was mentally and physically exhausted. Once the count was over for the night, I was able to lie down and rest well. Honestly, it was the best rest I had gotten in months. That's sad but true.

Everybody had to work in prison and I was told I had a week to get a job or they would place me wherever they saw fit. Of course, I immediately began looking for a job that wouldn't be too hard for me to do pregnant. I talked to the other inmates to find out what might be easier for me, I talked to a prison counselor. And, I ended up in the kitchen, where it was my job to cook for hundreds of women. I hated it because it was a lot of work, but it was better than cleaning or working in the wash room.

At least I was happy to know I would at least be getting paid.

But that happiness was short-lived when the guard said, "You'll be getting twelve cents an hour."

Twelve cents? Was that even legal?

"You could get a raise in a few months," the guard added, like she'd just told me something great. "After five years, you will be eligible to make a dollar an hour."

I just glared at her. I had no intention of being around in five years so that was useless information to me.

I settled into a routine of getting up at four-thirty in to make breakfast, wrapping up by noon, resting, then going to Bible study, the latter of which gave me the strength to face each new day.

I had time to think of how my life would be once I was released. I had the opportunity to start over again and I planned to do just that.

As days turned into nights, weeks into months, I found myself more lonely than ever. That's why I made sure I went to mail call. I'd go and I'd wait. And wait. And wait. Yet, my name was never called. No one was writing me. Eventually, I decided to stop torturing myself and skip mail call.

One day, after I'd been in prison for a couple of months, I was in my room reading, when one of the inmates walked up and said, "Hey, Alisha, they called your name in mail call."

I bolted upright.

"What, they did? Are you sure it was me?"

She laughed. "Yeah, girl."

I was excited and sad. Excited because finally, I had mail and sad, because once mail call was over, you had wait until the next day.

But I was unable to contain my excitement, so I went to the front to ask one of the guards who did the mail call, if there was any way I could get my mail early.

"Nope. You know the rules," the guard told me.

Dejected, I went back to my cell and fell asleep with dreams of what was in the mail for me. It really was sad how getting mail could become the highlight of my day.

The next day, I was the first one there for mail call. "Readus!" the mail clerk called out.

Like a scene out of a movie, I jumped in anticipation.

"Thank you," I mumbled as I grabbed the envelope and tore it open. I fell back against the wall when I saw the picture of my son, Ramon. He was so adorable and so cute, and it made my heart swell.

I showed everyone that picture and it really made my day. After that, I received several more pieces of mail from my mom and cousin. I really needed that correspondence because like I said, I had as lonely as I felt inside this prison. The emptiness that I had was unlike anything I ever imagined.

One thing that I discovered, though, was that I had a different relationship with the women than I expected. I came in expecting to be completely distrustful of the other women, and for a while, I was. But eventually, I found out that some of the women were like mothers of a church; they were caring and thoughtful, and eventually, broke down the wall that I had put up around me.

"Why don't you do your hair in a nice style, or put on make-up?" one of them asked me one day.

I thought about what she was saying and once again, I started having these feelings that I'd always had, but had worked so hard to suppress. Ever since I'd been in prison, I'd been having these long-ago buried feelings. I once again had a desire for women.

I had been attracted to women for as long as I could remember, but I never acted on my feelings because I knew that men were supposed to be the norm. Even still, my desire for women never went away.

But even though I was beginning to feel this way again, I was six months pregnant and the last thing I wanted was attention from a woman. What I'd discovered in prison, was that I was more of a lesbian than straight, but I wasn't attracted to anyone – man or woman – while I was pregnant.

Besides, a relationship was the last thing I needed at that time. My life was in a bad place. I needed God to help me learn how to trust in Him, I needed God to grow in me. So that is exactly what I was aiming for - growth and wisdom.

I was tired of the cycle of bad decisions. I'd been looking at life all wrong and needed to learn how to be responsible and not depend on others to do anything for me. What I needed to do was trust God enough to show me how to walk in this world alone.

Chapter 20

I started GED classes and continued to work from 4:30 am to noon in the kitchen. I kept my head low and stayed out of trouble. Time trickled by and as my stomach grew, so did my concern about delivering my baby in prison.

Since my arrival, I'd been trying, to no avail, to work out details about the MINT Program in Tallahassee, FL. I set an appointment with my caseworker to try and get to the bottom of this program that the warden had told me about.

"My baby is due in three weeks and I still haven't heard anything on the program," I told her.

"Well, I've been working on this, but I'm running into some problems," she replied. "Turns out, the only way you can go into the program is if someone in your family signs a form stating that they will take the baby after he or she is born."

"Wait, so I don't get to stay with my baby in the program?" My heart immediately began racing.

"This is just in case anything happens or you did something to get sent back to the prison before the end of the program. We have to have a backup plan for the baby."

I frowned. I had no intention on going back to prison. Ever. But I understood their reasoning. Since my time in prison would be almost up anyway by the time the program ended, I was sure that someone in my family would sign to take my child. Unfortunately, it wasn't as easy as I thought it would be.

My first call was to my mother.

"Mom, I need your help." I explained to her what I needed in order to stay in the program. "If I don't get someone to sign, the state will take my baby when he's three days old."

"Alisha, I can't raise any more children. I just can't," she said, her voice full with weariness.

"You won't have to raise him. You just sign, just in case," I cried.

"It's that just in case that I just can't take a chance on. You girls have put me through enough. I'm sorry. I just can't do it. You'll have to find someone else." Then, she hung up the phone.

I was devastated, but not shocked at my mother's reaction. The stress of all that we'd put my mother through had taken its toll. I knew I couldn't ask my aunt because she already had Ramon, and she would think the same way as my mother. So I turned to a close family member. I was sure that she would say yes since her son was grown.

I was floored at her response.

"Sorry," she said after I'd explained everything. "I'm just getting free of my responsibilities and I just don't want to take on another one."

I tried to explain to her that it was just a technicality. "It's just signing the paper so I can go into the program. You won't actually have to take my baby unless something happens."

"Yeah, it's that unless part that I have a problem with," she said, echoing my mother. "Sorry. You'll have to find someone else." Then, she, too, hung the phone up.

That broke my heart. It was only a few months before my release date. I couldn't understand why she wouldn't help me. I was angry and so hurt because it made no sense to me. Yes, I was the one in jail, and yes, I'd made the bad decision that put me in prison, but I needed help with my baby.

I knew that I couldn't wallow in my disheartenment for long. I had to keep working to find someone to sign the paper. So I called a church member, who had offered to "help any way she could, even taking the baby until I got out." Not only would she never accept my collect calls from prison, she refused to call back when I left messages and even when I had my caseworker leave a message.

Down, but not out, I called another friend and once again, explained the whole situation.

"Okay," my friend said when I was done with my spiel.

"Okay?" I wanted to jump for joy.

"Yes. But there's one catch," she replied.

That gave me pause.

"You have to agree to let me claim the baby on my income tax," she said.

My joy quickly faded. I'd worked before I was sent to prison, and was looking forward to filing my return when I got out.

"I can't do that," I said. "I'm gonna need that refund money to help me get back on my feet." I could sense the conversation shifting, so I quickly added, "But to be fair, you can claim my baby on your 2000 tax return." I was thinking next year would work better for me.

My friend got quiet, then replied. "Well, those are my terms. I claim your baby now, or I don't sign."

I couldn't believe I was being blackmailed! I finally agreed to sign the documents only because I needed to have someone sign my form for my unborn child. I really needed that security, that if anything went wrong, the baby would have someone to take care of him.

The next day, my friend faxed over a form to my caseworker, giving her permission to claim my son on her 1999 taxes. I signed it, then faxed it back to her.

"Now, we just wait on her to send back the form agreeing to take your baby," my caseworker told me.

I felt like a huge weight had been lifted off my shoulders. Only two days later, a boulder was placed right back on me. My caseworker called me back into her office.

"Alisha, have a seat."

The look on her face told me that she was about to deliver some bad news. I did as she instructed, never taking my eyes off of her.

"In all of my fifteen years working here, I've never seen a situation like this." Her eyes filled with disappointment. "Your friend has decided she won't sign the papers. She won't give us an explanation. She just said she's not doing it and to stop calling her."

Tears sprung to my eyes. The caseworker spent an hour comforting me, but ultimately, there was nothing either of us could do. Of course, I tried calling my friend, but she changed her phone number and I never talked to her again.

I had been struggling not to give up, but at that point, I was at the end of hope. I had lost faith in people, and was starting to lose faith in God.

"You need to pray and ask God to send you a solution," one of the elder prisoners told me one day after I'd been sitting by myself, crying for hours.

"I'm all prayed out," I sobbed.

"You never stop praying," she told me. "Those situations didn't work out because that's not where God wants your baby. We don't see that sometimes God places obstacles in our path to redirect us to the path that we really should be on." She flashed a warm smile, patted my cheek and walked off.

I thought about what she said. *Was there really someplace else my baby was supposed to be?* Considering time was flying by, if something didn't happen fast, there would be bigger problems. So there was nothing else that I could do but to trust God. I knew in my heart that God would not allow my baby to go into the state's custody. Once the state took a baby from a mother who was incarcerated, it was twice as hard to get the baby back.

I closed my eyes and prayed – I mean, really prayed for guidance.

Chapter 21

I often thought about my twin sister and wondered how she was doing and what was going on in her life while she was in prison. My sister accepted Christ right before we went to prison, and so considering she was a baby in Christ, my biggest concerns were that she would turn away from God, get resentment in her heart because she had to go to prison, and even turn away from me.

To my surprise, though, I got a letter from her, after not communicating for months.

In the first part of the letter, my sister said she had to get it approved for us to write to each other. I had been unable to get approved because Marisa had to go back to court because of her other case with Tamiko. She explained that Tamiko pled not guilty and the case went to trial and they called her into testify against her. Marisa also told me that so many things had happened - from her being on the plane for the first time, and how Tamiko sat in court lying, talking about it was Marisa who was the mastermind behind the whole scam.

It was so good to hear from her. I missed her so much. Even though we had our issues in the past, this was the first time we had been separated for such an extended amount of time.

Within that letter, Marisa gave me some information that would change the course of my time in prison. Marisa explained that she asked the judge for an extra day because getting exactly twelve months in prison meant that we had to do the entire time, but with the extra day it would take time off of our sentence. When we first got sentenced, our sentence was twelve months to the date, which blocked us from receiving any good time. Had we been sentenced to twelve months and one day, we would have been in a position to receive good time, which means that our sentence could be reduced by good behavior.

Once I had all of the information and the documents, I sent the letter out as well and I patiently waited for a response. I prayed that God would grant me the same favor He had given my sister.

I calculated the time of when I would give birth, and if a miracle happened, I would be released before the MINT program ended. (So it was a true blessing the day that I got the letter stating that I was approved for the extra day and they were able to take over a month off of my sentence because of the extra day. What a difference a day makes because now my new release day would be Sept. 16, 2000.

I cried tears of joy because I knew that God did it. If God did that for me, I knew that he had a plan for my baby.

I got to see God's plan the day one of the women on my floor walked up and asked me, "Hey, when is your baby due?"

I rubbed my stomach and smiled. "In May."

"Oh, I thought I heard you don't get out until September."

"I don't." I lost my smile as I explained my situation to her.

She stood there and listened to me with her heart. She always was willing to lend an ear and prayer to the women in the prison. So as I begin to explain the situation to Michelle, she looked at me and stated, "Everything is going to be all right; just trust God."

A few days later, Michelle came over to me as I sat on my bed and said, "I have someone who can sign your paper."

I bolted upright. "What! Are you serious?"

She smiled. "Yes, I sure am. I will be calling her in the next five minutes and I wanted you to have the opportunity to speak to her so that you can explain your situation to her in more detail."

Within five minutes, my life changed. The woman, Mrs. Johnson went to church with Michelle. She explained that Michelle had asked for her to lift me up in prayer about what was going on.

"It was at that time I knew that it was destined for me to sign your form so that you can go to the MINT program to be with your baby," she said.

I burst into tears again – only this time, they were tears of joy.

Early the next morning, I could not wait to go and speak to my caseworker to tell her the good news. She spoke with Mrs. Johnson and within three days, everything was set.

The only thing that needed to be done was for me to get the exact date I would be leaving to go to the program. I was so excited and grateful to finally have some good news in my life.

The prison ministry gifted me with clothes to take on my journey to Tallahassee, where the MINT program was based. Luckily when you are in the MINT program, you can wear regular clothes. The ministry also promised that once I got settled in Tallahassee, they would make sure my baby had food and clothing as well.

I finally felt good about my life. And I was grateful that God had shown up and showed out on my behalf. Favor had fallen on my life and God was providing all of my needs.

The day came when it was time for me to head to the MINT program. Once I made it to the front so that I could depart, I was informed that I had a check for my kitchen work – a whole $15, plus an extra $20 from the prison. My caseworker had also gotten me two maternity outfits for my trip.

I said my last goodbyes and gave several women a hug before leaving. I looked at Michelle with tears in my eyes and said "Thank you so much; if you didn't pray for me and contact Mrs. Johnson this couldn't be."

Her warm smile told me how happy she was to help, then I hugged her one last time.

I boarded the van, looked back and I mumbled, "This part is over."

The two people that transported me to Tallahassee were my case worker and a guard from the prison. I was like a kid on her first road trip, I was so giddy with excitement.

I smiled when the van sped by a McDonald's, a gas station, a mall-- so many things that I used to take for granted.

"Are you hungry?" the caseworker asked once we'd been riding about two hours.

"Yes! Very." I rubbed my stomach. "Both of us are starving."

"What do you want?"

"McDonalds," I replied.

"Really, McDonalds?"

"Yes!" It may have seemed small to them, but it was a very big deal to me.

Once we arrived in Tallahassee, the caseworker pointed to a fast food restaurant right up the street from our facility.

"You can walk there if you want to. You just have to get permission from the person in charge at this facility."

Really? I couldn't believe it. Despite me being imprisoned, God had granted me favor to live as if I was free!

When we got on the property, we headed straight to an office to meet the program director. She explained what was expected of me and what would be done within the next few weeks. The first thing I had to do was see the OB/GYN doctor. Then, I had to get on Medicaid and sign up for the WIC program.

I was excited about qualifying for Medicaid, a program for women with no income/low income to be able to get health insurance, as well as the WIC program, which is designed to assist in getting healthy food while you are pregnant.

But the program director really made my day when she informed me that I would be permitted to attend church away from the facility once a week on Sundays from 9am to 2pm. For me, this was a breath of fresh air because I really wanted to continue to go to church. I enjoyed reading about God and I wanted to continue growing.

"You'll also be able to visit CVS and other stores in the area," the director added. "But only with good behavior."

She didn't have to worry about me. I was going to be on my best behavior! No way was I going to mess up and get kicked out of the MINT program.

After I'd gone through the formalities and got settled in, my caseworker asked, "So, what do you plan to do first?"

"I would love to go to the beauty supply store," I told her. I know that may have seemed like an awkward request, but I loved my weave and I desperately needed to fix it up. These last six months had been murder on my hair. Besides, there was a college right behind the facility where I was staying and well, you just never knew who you might meet!

When I was locked up, I really didn't care how I looked, but now that I felt free (even though technically, I was not), I wanted to look beautiful again.

So once I'd gotten permission, me and some of the other ladies from the program headed to the Beauty Supply store and CVS to grab a few personal items like soap, deodorant, lotion and cocoa butter for my stomach. While I was at CVS, I met a lady who asked me "When is your baby due?"

"May 15th," I replied. I also told her that I was in the MINT program up the street.

"What's that?" she asked.

"It's a place for incarcerated mothers to go to give birth."

She didn't seem fazed that I just admitted to being a convicted felon. She began to share part of her life with me. Her name was Sharon and her testimony was beautiful. Sharon told me that she had gotten into a horrible car accident, and they expected her to never walk again. She encouraged me with me the faith that she had, despite what she went through. She had been to therapy and had to learn to walk again. My heart went out to her and it made me think of my life and how God could work a miracle in so many different ways. Her story gave me hope, and I was so thankful that

I met her. As we continued to talk, she asked me, "Do they allow you to go to church?"

"Yes," I replied.

"Well, I'd love to invite you to my church," she said. "I can come pick you up. I stay only a few blocks from here so it wouldn't be a problem for me to swing through and get you."

Although I knew nothing about this lady, I instantly knew that God had placed her in my life.

Sharon and I exchanged numbers and were able to set up the first Sunday when I would attend her church. After we finished talking, the other girls and I headed back. Unlike when I first arrived at the prison in Marianna, I started bonding with the women immediately. I don't know if it was the fact that we all were pregnant or what, but we sat for hours and talked about our pregnancies. All of the women shared the fact that once they had their babies and the three months were up, they'd have to go back to prison to finish their time. I was the only one who did not have to return to the prison after my son was born, and I felt so bad for the other ladies because I knew it would be hard.

The next morning, I saw that one of the ladies who had walked to the store with us was missing from breakfast. I figured that she must have gone to an appointment and would be back later.

"Where's Tammy?" I asked one of the other girls when she still wasn't there by noon.

"Tammy's gone."

I frowned. "Gone where?"

"Back to prison," the girl replied.

"Prison? Why?"

The girl shook her head in pity. "Well, her boyfriend picked her up from the prison, and they were supposed to have come straight here, but they didn't. On the way, they stopped at a hotel and yesterday the Feds found out about it. They took her around three this morning."

My mouth dropped open in shock. Since I didn't have anyone

to pick me up and transport me to Tallahassee, I didn't even know that getting a personal ride was even an option.

I felt awful for Tammy. Her decision to put a man before herself had caused her to lose this great opportunity.

The fact that she had to go back to prison had to be a harsh reality for Tammy. It was definitely a wake-up call for anyone even thinking about doing something wrong.

I was still thinking about Tammy when the program director called to tell me that I had a package up front. That was strange since no one in my family even knew where I was, so I had no idea who could be sending me anything.

Once I retrieved and opened my package, I smiled when I saw it was from the church that was at the prison. They kept their word and I had brand new clothes, pajamas to sleep in, underwear, bras, socks, and shoes. I was so grateful. God truly did supply all of your needs. I had everything I needed to continue to grow into my last trimester.

During my first week, I went to the doctor for my prenatal care. During my visit, they did all of the normal procedures that needed to be done to insure that the mother and baby were doing well. I went to my WIC appointment and Medicaid appointment within that same week. And on Sunday, Sharon came and picked me up for church as she had promised.

The next week began and I got a phone call from the doctor's office that sent ripples of fear through my body.

"Your pap smear was abnormal, so we need to set up a biopsy to see if there are any other major problems," the nurse told me.

Although I had faith, I was nervous. I was scared for my baby and scared for me. Suppose they found something that would prevent me from seeing my children grow up?

I went in for the biopsy. "This may be a bit uncomfortable," the doctor told me. "And you may experience some bleeding, but it should go away in a few days."

A bit uncomfortable was the understatement of the decade. It was downright painful, but I made it through. And three days later, my worst fears were realized when the doctor called me back to break the news.

"It looks you are in the first stages of cervical cancer," he said.

I immediately began crying, but the doctor gave me some comfort when he added, "It sounds worse than it is. You are in the early stages, which can be treated with the proper medication."

Suddenly, it dawned on me that had I still been at the prison in Marianna, I might never have gotten the pap smear, and hence, never would have caught the cancer in time. Once again, God had come through for me.

That was just one more thing to bolster my faith while I served my time.

Chapter 22

I continued to see my doctor as I anxiously awaited the delivery of my son. The doctor had informed me that I might have to have a C-section because the baby appeared to be very big. He also said they might have to induce labor earlier than my due date because of the size of the baby.

I was able to call Jonathan and tell him the delivery date. I prayed that he would meet me at the hospital, but with him, I just never knew.

I guess he was feeling emotional because he seemed insulted that I even thought that he might not be there. And not only did he assure me he'd be there, but he began to harass me about getting back together.

"Babe, I love you and I want us to work this out," he said. "This time without you has made me really miss you."

He didn't realize that my mind was made up, and I was not going back down the same road I'd been down before with him. Prison had changed me and I was determined to stay focused on more positive things and to live my life better than before.

Jonathan sent me some money a few times, so I could get items for the baby. I really believe that he thought by doing that, he would change my mind about us getting back together. For me, I saw his gestures as things he was supposed to be doing anyway.

It lasted for a little while, but it didn't take long for the real Jonathan to re-emerge. When I didn't do things his way, he began to act as horrible as he always acted. He picked the worst day to come out of the box: my delivery date.

I was already in severe pain, and did not have any room for

arguments. Jonathan consistently called up to the hospital talking bad to me.

"How do I even know that's my baby?" he snapped on me during one of my brutal contractions. "You're a hoe, so that could be anybody's baby."

I believed in natural childbirth, so I was in extreme pain and very uncomfortable.

"You FUCKED up and now I'm missing the birth of my child," he said, like he hadn't just questioned the paternity two seconds ago. "If you weren't in prison, you would not have to go through this by yourself; you did this to yourself."

The last thing I needed was a guilt trip, but Jonathan didn't care. He just went on and on.

It got so bad that I had to tell the nurses to stop all phone calls to my room. I was getting stressed out and all I could do was cry. I felt so alone and like no one cared. My family members treated me like I didn't exist or like I was going to be in prison forever, and my baby daddy was like Dr. Jekyll and Mr. Hyde.

It was very sad that I had to go through this alone with no one by my side, except for the program director. I labored without any pain medicine for two days.

On the third day, the doctor said, "Since you are not due yet, we will let you go home until your body goes into labor naturally." This was very frustrating to hear because if my baby was the size of a full term baby now, what would happen if we continued to wait until my body naturally went into labor? Considering my last baby was two weeks late, it a good reason for concern. Not to add the size of this baby could be dangerous.

Time passed on and that day never came. The doctor went on vacation and came back, but I still hadn't gone into labor. . Once again, we discussed trying to induce labor. If that didn't work they would have to do a C-Section.

On May 31, 2000, I went back into the hospital. They induced me again and the process started at 10 a.m. Active labor did not start until 4:00 p.m. By 7:00 p.m. it was time to push. My son, Romel, was finally here. He'd entered the world weighing 9 lbs., 2 ounces.

After a day in the hospital, my son and I returned to the program and I continued a non-eventful existence – trying to keep my head low, take care of my son, and reach my release date without any trouble.

My son was growing at a rapid rate, and I was enjoying the chance to not do anything else and just be a mom. With my previous children, I'd gone back to work pretty quickly, so I didn't have that bonding time. I was able to get that with Romel and for me, it was just an indication of all the good things that were to come.

Chapter 23

Freedom was right around the corner. And I almost let it slip from my grasp – all because of a woman with an attitude.

Amanda Davis was one of those women in the MINT program who was always complaining about something. She was one of those women who talked about everyone and everything. She also thought she was some kind of super mom – even though this was her first child and she was still pregnant.

One day, Amanda decided that she would tell me what I was doing wrong with my son. Since she first arrived at the MINT program, she had a negative view of people and always had something to say about somebody's parenting skills. It was funny considering she had never given birth to a child at the time, nor did she know what being a parent was about; she could only go on what she thought she knew.

Before she had her baby, she would often criticize me about how much my baby cried. There were times when I tried to explain to her that when a baby cried, that was their way of communicating with us. The baby could be bored, hungry, sick or just frustrated, but that was the only way for the baby to communicate.. Romel apparently had a lot to say because he did cry all the time. He was one of the loudest babies in the program.

I had finally gotten Romel to sleep one morning and was in the dining area of the building, warming up his bottle for when he woke up. Amanda was watching TV, but other than that, the room was pretty quiet. I left out for a minute and when I was heading back into the room, something told me to stand outside of the door when I heard voices.

"That wench knows she should've stayed in here while this bottle was warming up. She's gonna burn that poor baby. And to think, she has other kids."

I didn't know who Amanda was talking to, but I definitely recognized her voice.

Fed up, I entered, ignoring the woman who must've come into the room after I left.

"Amanda, I am about sick of your big ass mouth," I snapped. "Every time I walk out of the room, you have something to say. Well, here is your chance to say it to my face."

As I figured, she just stood there looking stupid because she could talk the talk while someone's back was turned, but could not face the music when the person was right in front of her face.

I walked closer to her. "Say it now," I growled.

She began to stutter as she saw the anger in my eyes. Looking back, I know I overreacted, but I was on edge because my release date was approaching. That should have been a good thing, but I was stressed because as the time became closer, I was facing serious issues. I had nowhere to go once I was released, I had no money, no support, and I felt like I was about to explode. It was time for someone to pay for the hell I had endured being locked up these last nine months.

So she volunteered herself when she started trouble by running her big mouth. At least that's what I was thinking. Everyone gets to that breaking point, and I was there, and she was the bull's eye.

"You don't scare me," she said, stepping even closer to me.

Before I knew it, I had grabbed her neck and flung her to the ground. We were in full-on fighting mode, with me trying to stuff her into the microwave right alongside my baby's bottle.

We'd only been fighting for a minute when the new director came running in with about three other people. Just as I was about to smash her head into the floor, the director said, "Think about what you're doing, Alisha!"

That caused me to stop mid-smash. *Oh, my, God. What was I*

doing?

I stepped back. The director's words were a slap back to reality, not only for me, but for Amanda as well because she stood up and backed away, too.

"Ummm, we-we were just playing around," Amanda quickly said.

The director shot a side eye at her and pointed to her office.

"In my office, now," she told me.

She had such a disappointed expression across her face. She had believed in me and now, I was so ashamed.

"What in the world were you thinking?" the director asked me. "I expect this from Amanda, but not from you. Do you know this can get you sent back to prison?"

"I, we, I mean, we were just wrestling," I stammered, following the story that Amanda had started.

"Girl, don't play with me," she said.

Tears sprung to the forefront. "It's just. . . I'm so scared. I get out in two weeks and I have nowhere for me and my son to go."

She released a sympathetic sigh. "I understand that, but you are responsible for your own actions."

"I know," I softly replied.

"You know I have to tell your probation office what happened, right?"

That felt like a punch to my gut. I couldn't go back to prison. I just couldn't!

I may have felt bad, and I may have felt sorry, but that didn't matter. Not when my probation officer got on the phone. "How am I supposed to trust your judgment with you choosing to act out two weeks prior to your release?" she yelled at me when the caseworker handed me the phone. "Your family was right, you're a lost cause!"

I don't know what hurt more – the fact that I'd jeopardized my freedom over a fight, or that my family had talked that way about me to my probation officer.

Even though my probation officer had just berated me, at least having her on the phone gave me the opportunity to ask, "Can you help me get into a shelter?" Then, I explained my situation to her. "There's a shelter about 45 minutes outside of Birmingham, but I need your permission to be there," I said, deciding that at that very moment, the most important thing was finding someplace for me and my baby to go.

She didn't hesitate in her response. "No. I don't want you that far away considering what a troublemaker you are."

I hung up from that call and left the director's office dejected and despondent. Over the next few days, my caseworker and I worked hard, trying to find a place for me and my baby to go. Marisa had been sent to work release in June 2000 and she was fortunate to work and find a place and we considered where she lived , but the place where she lived did not have children. It was a transitional home for single women only, and the family floor within the facility did not have any rooms. So I contacted a shelter right in Birmingham to see if they would have any openings within the next few weeks. I explained to them that I would be getting released from prison on September 16th and that I had three sons that I would be bringing with me.

I was ecstatic when they said they would find room. I was even more ecstatic when my probation officer agreed that I could go there.

Finally, I had a sense of peace. At least I had a place to stay and I would be with all of my children. As I sat back on the bed thinking of all of the things that I wanted to do and the goals that needed to be set in place to be successful in life, it dawned on me, my life was picking up from where it stopped a year ago.

As I prepared to leave, I informed Jonathan of the day and time that we would be making it into Birmingham so that he could see his son. Of course, he still thought he had a chance to get back with me, but after all that he'd put me through, that was not going to happen. It was time to be about my business, and there was no man or anyone who was going to stop that no matter what they said or did. I had a renewed determination for my children, for me. I was not the only one who paid for the crime that I committed. My children, my mother, and my aunt who had to watch my son paid for my crimes as well. So I had to make sure that the time I spent away from my family was not in vain.

It was funny -- on my release date -- I was the only one left in the program. All the other women had gone back to prison and their absence made me realize how blessed I really was.

Although I was emotional about leaving, I was excited as well. In a matter of hours, I would see Rashard and Ramon, after so long. I wondered how they would respond to seeing me, what they would do, and if Ramon, who was only one when I left, even remembered me.

"You ready?"

The program manager's voice snapped me out of my thoughts.

"Beyond ready," I replied, standing to grab my baby, who was still sleeping.

I said my goodbyes to the director of the program and the assistant, and headed out to my fresh start.

As we rode to the bus station, there was so much running through my head, but the one reason for me to rejoice was the fact that this was over.

Tears started to flow and my emotions were so high, but my energy was just as high. My mother and twin sister were going to be at the bus station in Birmingham waiting for me.

As the bus pulled up at the station in downtown Birmingham, I saw Rashard, Marisa, my mother, Jonathan, and my probation officer waiting for me to get off the bus. As I gathered my things, I started to cry. Finally I was about to have freedom - freedom to live, freedom to go to a restaurant, freedom to be a mother. And most importantly, freedom of choice, the power to choose never to return to prison again.

I had finally broken through the bars in my life because I accepted my mistakes, I was taking responsibility. I made up my mind to live life to benefit my children, not to benefit my wants, and to also be wise in my choices. I recognized that it was in my hands to live my life with purpose and on purpose.

Chapter 24

After I arrived at the bus station and was reunited with my family, I headed straight over to the shelter, ready to settle into my new life.

My probation officer met me there and she gave me the rundown of my responsibilities while on probation for the next three years: Secure a job within the first month, don't buy anything or move without getting approval from her. I was cool with all of her guidelines. I was just grateful to be free.

After I completed all the paperwork, I was just ready to get my kids settled. Then a caseworker walked in to the shelter and dropped a bombshell.

"I'm sorry, there is not enough room for you and three children," she informed me. "We only have room for two of your kids."

I was devastated, especially because my mom had just told me my son "couldn't stay with her another night." She said she didn't know what she'd been thinking, but she was just too old to continue caring for him. I was expecting my aunt from Huntsville to arrive at the shelter with Ramon in tow any minute now. What was I supposed to tell her?

Both me and my probation officer tried to get the shelter director to change her mind, but at first she wouldn't budge. We kept telling her that I had no other options.

"She will be on the street with her children," the probation officer said.

"I will," I agreed. "And, I had cleared this with you. You told me that I could be here."

It took us almost an hour, but finally the shelter director said that she'd see what she could do. As I waited I wondered what was going to happen to me and my sons. We really would be on the street if we couldn't stay at this shelter.

When she returned, she told me that she'd worked something out and my children and I were able to stay.

We rested well that night. The next morning after we ate breakfast, I started to look for job. First, I had to get my resume together and the shelter had an office where I was able to put it together. Then, I went to work. It took me a week, but I found a job. And all three of my children were in daycare.

Before I started working, though, I wanted to handle some business about Rashard at the Social Security office. He'd gotten approved for SSI before I left, and I just wanted to make sure that everything was okay.

Once I made it to the Social Security office, I explained to the worker that I had been in prison for the last year and that Rashard was back in my custody.

I also had the paperwork from my mother stating that Rashard was with me, so the payee needed to be changed.

After looking over everything, the worker at the Social Security office said, "It looks like there was a check for your son that was never mailed."

"Really?"

She nodded. "So that means this back check will be coming to you."

"How much is it for?" I asked.

When she told me, I almost fell out. I would be getting a check in the amount of $3,500 dollars within three to six weeks. There was paperwork that needed to be signed in order for me to become the payee for his check and that would start the process to release the money to me.

Of course, I was shocked. I walked ten miles back to the shelter. I truly didn't give the distance any thought, I just walked, cried, and gave God praise.

While I was ecstatic about that check, I could not wait to start making money. Once I explained to my probation officer that I had gotten a job, and gave her the date I was going to start, she stated that she had never seen anyone get a job the first week they were released from prison. In my eyes there was no time to play; my future and the future of my children were in my hands.

I started my job and was there for about a month, when I began looking for a place to stay. I was unsure of where I wanted to live, I just knew that I was not about to be at the shelter any longer than I had to be. I applied for several apartments and finally got approved for a two-bedroom apartment. My rent was going to be $199 a month. The apartment wasn't much, but it was going to be mine. My children would have a place to call home.

The check from Social Security finally arrived and I started spending that $3500 in my head, making plans like it was $35,000. I had so many things I wanted to do. Paying for that apartment was one of them. I also needed to get a new car.

After getting my probation officer's approval (which I had to do on almost everything), I bought a 1996, 5 speed, with leather interior, fully-loaded sedan.

After I purchased, it, I parked the car up the street from the shelter and headed in. One of the ladies at the shelter saw me and told the caseworker about my new car.

The caseworker was pissed; I honestly believe that she was mad at me for the drive and determination I had for my life. I'm sure she'd had a lot of women come there with no focus and no determination, but maybe they didn't have the reasons I had to get it together. I had lost everything and it was up to me to make a comeback.

The caseworker contacted my probation officer about my car. I'm sure she was hoping to get me in trouble for making a large purchase without permission.

I wish I could've seen the look on her face when my probation officer explained that she already knew.

God was on my side and the woman hated it so much, but she had to get over herself. It was really funny to me how people said they wanted the best for me, but in reality, they're fine with me doing well, as long as I wasn't doing better than them.

I had every intention of doing better than everyone I knew who was a convicted felon, because I was not about to let my past dictate my future.

I was ecstatic when the day came for me to move into my apartment. That day came on October 25, 2000. I packed up everything that belonged to me and my sons and left them in my room. Considering that I had several trips to make, I decided it would be more efficient if I took one load to my apartment, then return to the shelter to get the rest of my things.

Once I got back there, though, I noticed that a couple of my bags were missing. I was more sad than upset about it. It was just sad that those women hated my drive that much that they would steal from me.

I wasn't going to allow anyone to get away with that, though; I went downstairs and informed the director that someone had stolen from me and they needed to do something to fix the situation.

The director did not initially believe me. But, then I told her, "I want to call the police."

Of course, she didn't want that, so she got up off her fat behind to go investigate.

I don't know what she said to the group of women who had gathered in the living room, but my things began to magically reappear.

But then, right before I left, the director said to me, "You can't come on our property again!"

I almost asked her why was I the one being banned? Then, it dawned on me, I didn't really care. As far as I was concerned, I would never see this place again anyway. So, I just said goodbye and went on my way.

Chapter 25

We finally made it to the apartment and for the first time in a year, I was able to stay out past six p.m. It was really amazing to see how God moved in my favor - down to the furniture in my apartment.

I got a king sized bed, dressers, bunk beds, living room furniture, a TV and a stove, all for $150. Not only did I have a house, I had a home.

Some people would not be grateful for a place that looked so unpleasant on the outside, but I was not only grateful, I was content. I remembered something our Sunday School teacher used to tell us when I was a little girl: *Be content in whatever situation you are in and watch God bless you even more.*

I could not believe that my life had taken such a drastic turn, but what was more amazing was the fact that I learned how to depend on God and learn where true freedom came from. True freedom comes from the inner most part of you. Despite the fact I was a prisoner in prison, I learned that my freedom was not just physical, but it was mental as well.

I had lived in prison in my mind, not recognizing that I could achieve anything I wanted if I used what I naturally had, and that was determination, and focus. I had to focus on the things that were most important to me, and let that be my driving fuel to my destination. It's easy to say what you can't do until you have to do it. In the end, I won favor with God because God was all I had to depend and to be honest, God was the only one I needed in the first place.

Trusting in people is a set-up for failure, but trusting in God is a set-up for success.

Throughout my journey, I had favor along the way: with my social worker in prison, in the MINT program, and in looking for a job and daycare. I broke through the bars that were in my life.

I was proud that for the first time really, I was learning to live life independently, without being defined by a man, by money, or by any relationship status. I realized what I had been accepting in my life was not acceptable. The love that I had been seeking was a love that I had to first acquire within myself.

Choosing change and choosing to live life in the midst of the sadness and sorrow can give you a strength that you never thought you had. I didn't know I had it until I hit rock bottom. It was at that point that I realized I had two options, stay down or get up. When you recognize that having faith is all you have, you learn to trust God more than man. Even when we can't see it, God is working things out for the good.

The entire time I had been in prison God did things that I thought people could do for me, or *should* do for me. But God chose to show me who He was by removing me from the people I knew and trusted. That's what I believe my prison stay was all about. God used that time to really show me that He wanted me to learn to depend on Him. Yes, it has been a hard journey, and I can say that through it all, I did experience hurt and pain. But one thing is for sure – and that's that this journey has truly been worth it.

MARISA

LIVING IN THE BLINDERS OF
DECEPTION AND GREED

Chapter 26

My life was different from my twin sister. I was married to a man when I was 18 years old who seemed to love my unborn child and me. I was four months pregnant when I met Gerald and he came in like my black knight. It never mattered to him that I was pregnant with another man's child, nor that that man left me when I was five weeks pregnant.

Although I quit school, was pregnant, and had nothing going for myself, it didn't matter to Gerald. I often thought to myself, "What the hell is wrong with him?" I couldn't figure it out because he was there for me from the beginning and that was something that I wasn't used to.

Gerald was smart, focused, and goal oriented, and he was in the military. I met him when Alisha and I went to visit one of her friends on Red Stone Arsenal in Huntsville, Alabama.

Gerald was there at Alisha's friend's house, sitting quietly, watching a football game. He was so quiet I didn't realize he was in the room until at least thirty minutes later. He looked up, smiled, and returned to watching television.

Alisha and I hung out at her friends for a little while longer and then left. Two weeks later, Alisha invited her friend over for dinner.

"I'd love to come," he replied. "But can I bring Gerald, you know that dude that was over my house when you guys came over a few weeks ago. He's new to the area and doesn't really know anyone."

"Yes," Alisha quickly replied.

I wanted to ask why the hell he was coming over. I hoped she wasn't getting any bright ideas about fixing me up, especially since

I was four months pregnant at the time.

Less than twenty minutes after their arrival, my indifference to Gerald disappeared. I was fascinated by his intelligence. His words captivated me and when he talked abut his goals, he inspired me. He had such a positive outlook. On top of that, he was really nice.

At one point, while he was talking, I had to catch myself and come back to reality.

A man like that wouldn't want a woman like you.

The voice inside my head tried to get me to give up any idea of taking things any further than that conversation on that day. But something about me made Gerald want to know more about me. After dinner we sat and talked and his kindness helped me to escape my doubts. He told me about how he was from Texas and that he worked in the surgery room at the hospital on the base. We talked and talked, never seeming to come to a stopping point.

Although I was not married, neglected, and pregnant, I opened up and shared my experiences with him. And, he took it all in with an open heart. After that night, he pursued me, stayed consistent, and married me five months later.

The makings of a beautiful love story. . . only it was far from that.

By month six, that warm, loving man I fell in love with disappeared, and in his place came an emotionally abusive man who got off by tearing me down. It didn't help that I had a bad temper when provoked, and Gerald was suddenly in the business of provoking me. Our relationship turned volatile very quickly.

I didn't know how to handle negative emotions so I responded to his insults the only way I knew how – with violence. I threw things at him, I even fought him like I was a man, too.

I didn't understand why he was being so mean to me when I loved him so much. I did whatever he asked, waking up every morning to cook breakfast, and sexing him crazy every night. What did I do so wrong that would lead him to treat me this way?

After a while I got tired of the fighting, fussing, cussing, downgrading, and low self-esteem that came from the way he treated me. If he wanted to believe I was worthless, I was going to show him.

My first choice came just a day after my decision to show him. I was at the auto shop getting my truck checked out because the soft top wouldn't stay down.

As soon as I walked in the shop, a man looking like the poster boy for Mr. Goodstuff walked up to me.

"How may I help you?"

I was lost in his fineness. He was wrapped up in work clothes, work boots, and buffness. My eyes scanned every inch of his frame.

"Hello?" he repeated.

"Sorry," I said, snapping myself out of my trance. "I'm having trouble with my Jeep. The soft top won't stay down." I pointed outside to my car.

He looked at me and smiled. "I can help you with that."

I smiled back. "I would appreciate that."

I followed him outside as he went to work. Those muscles were to die for, and lustful thoughts filled my mind. If my husband knew what I was doing, he probably would have killed me. I was most definitely playing in tough territory, but the energy between us was amazing.

He introduced himself as Terrance and I studied him some more. Terrance had the most beautiful chocolate skin, broad shoulders, buff arms, and a swag that said "I know I look good." He should have had on a shirt that said "Delightful Temptation" because that's exactly what he was.

I glanced at my marquise cut diamond ring and decided that no matter how bad things were at home, this man was trouble so I would just thank him and leave. Which I did.

But two weeks later, Terrance was still on my brain. And Gerald was giving me every reason to seek him out. After one especially violent argument, that's exactly what I did.

I suddenly decided it was time for my oil change (or maybe it wasn't). Either way, I needed to see him again, so I stopped by and we talked a little. But I still couldn't get up the nerve to let him know I was interested.

Two days later, I heard a ticking in my car, and of course, Terrance was the only one who could help me. So, I headed back to the auto shop.

"Back again?" he said when I pulled up. His smile let me know he was happy to see me.

"Yes, I'm wondering if you're tampering with my truck to keep me coming back," I said flirtatiously.

He laughed. "I didn't, but that's a good idea. Let me see what I can mess up so you can come back tomorrow."

That was my cue. "How about I come back on one of your days off?"

He stood up, stared at me to see if I was serious. When he determined that I was, he said, "I'm off Friday. Can I see you?"

"I'd like that," I said.

He nodded his approval, then jiggled a few wires under my hood. "The ticking should be fixed and I can't wait until Friday."

"See you then," I said. I couldn't believe how giddy with excitement I was.

Thankfully, Gerald and I were barely speaking, so he wasn't able to spoil my mood when I got home, nor for the next few days. When Friday arrived, I waited until Gerald left for work, and then I put on my flyest outfit: black boots, black boot cut jeans, a gold shirt that showed a little cleavage. The outfit made my entire five-foot-seven, size twelve frame, pop.

The most unfortunate, yet convenient circumstance was that I worked at night at a hospital, and my husband worked at a another hospital during the day. It gave me too much time to play and do wrong.

And right about now, I was ready to do wrong. I'd told myself I wasn't going to *really* cheat. I just wanted to spend a little time away from home because I was so emotionally hurt and starving for attention and appreciation.

Terrance and I sat and talked as we ate pizza. He told me that he was involved with someone, but he was miserable just like me. Neither of us even understood why we stayed.

Then, our talk turned to music. The music played and we reminisced on old school jams. Suddenly, one of my favorite songs came on, Tony Terry "When I'm With You" and Terrance stood and took my hand.

"Dance with me," he said.

I thought about all that body against me, and knew all my promises to not really cheat were about to go out the window.

I didn't say a word as I stood and let him pull me close. I pushed aside all thoughts of how wrong this was. But I couldn't help it. Being with Terrance made me feel loved. And appreciated. And safe. He wasn't laughing at me, or talking about me, he was just happy to be with me.

As the song came to an end, I knew that this date needed to end, too. It was the only way I wouldn't end up in the bed with him.

I pulled back. "This has been great, but I really need to go."

He looked disappointed. "I understand, but can I get a hug before you go?"

I didn't say a word as I stepped into his strong embrace. His Hugo Boss cologne ran up my nose as he slowly kissed my neck.

Run NOW!

My conscience kicked in...but that neglected part of me kicked it to the curb and the next thing I knew, my gold blouse was coming off in the living room at his sister's house, I only prayed she wouldn't come busting through the door and catch me with my legs on his shoulders because it was about to go down. At this point my boots, my pants, then my red lace underwear were coming off.

I was a married woman about to make love to another man. And I'd never felt better.

Chapter 27

Terrance became my medicine. He was the one who took away my pain, who comforted me out of my sadness, and who gave me my high when I was low.

Gerald remained oblivious to my cheating ways. He continued to degrade me and sometimes I would smile inside, thinking of the good loving Terrance had just given me.

The thoughts and memories of Terrance kept me smiling, but it was still overwhelming battling with Gerald.

One day Gerald tried to take the keys to my car and I was fed up with his controlling ways. So when he snatched my keys and ran out the door, I ran right behind him and picked up the top of the barbecue grill. All I could think was 'Enough is enough. This motherfucker is going down today.'

When Gerald jumped into his car, I started banging on the window with the grill top, screaming, "Get the fuck out the car!"

The neighbors were looking, but I didn't care. Gerald couldn't stand a scene, so he got out the car and stomped back in the house. I was screaming as I followed him.

"Give me my keys!"

The argument intensified and my anger felt like it was coming to a boil.

"I'm so sick of your ignorant ass," he screamed back at me. "That's why don't nobody want you!"

That was it. I ran into the kitchen and grabbed a butcher knife.

"I'm tired of you!" I yelled as I lunged toward him. He took off, running down the hall and into the bathroom. I banged on the door. Of course he wouldn't open it, so with the knife, I started cutting the door.

Once I pried it open some, I leaned back and kicked the door in. He was shocked and I took that moment as an opportunity to jump on him, knocking him into the tub.

When I landed on top of him, I screamed, "I hate you! I should kill you!"

Tears streamed down my face. I looked like a madwoman, but I was just fed up.

"Marisa! Stop. What are you doing? Get off me," he shouted, as he struggled to keep me from slashing him with the knife.

Of course, since Gerald was so much bigger than me, it didn't take much for him to overpower me. He pushed me off of him, then tossed me aside like I was nothing more than a rag doll. I landed on the floor and just started sobbing.

"This is that dumb shit I'm talking about," he said as he pulled himself out of the tub. "And you wonder why I'm not attracted to your fat ass."

I laid on that floor and just cried. I cried from the abuse. I cried because I wondered what had happened to that strong black woman that I believe I once was. I cried because I wanted to be with Terrance. I cried because I didn't want this, I was tired of sitting in my jeep in the parking lot of our apartment complex smoking a black & mild dreading going into the house with him, I was tired of his mean ways, and I was tired of lying to Gerald to be with Terrance, I was just tired of not being good enough.

Gerald walked out of the bathroom, but I just laid there for awhile. Finally I pulled myself together, and decided that the emotional abuse was making me crazy. I deserved better than this.

That next week I left Gerald, but what was surprising is that I left Terrance, too. I didn't want to see him anymore either. I left Terrance because I knew I was no good for neither one of them. I was burnt out on love, caring, support, it was my time to live!

Although Terrance was disappointed that I was leaving, he understood. He and I saw each other a few more times after I left, but as time passed on, he faded from my mind. He was now a thing of my past.

Chapter 28

When I left Gerald I didn't realize how much anger, resentment, emptiness, and brokenness I was carrying with me. All I knew was that I was twenty-one, single, hot, and free. This would be the first time I was an adult woman playing by my own rules. I didn't have to go home to anyone, and I knew I would not let anyone hurt me again. I was in control of my life now, and no man was going to stop me.

I moved back home with my mom in Birmingham, Alabama and unleashed the beast within. I did whatever I wanted with whomever I wanted - including married men. To me, married men were safe; they didn't need full-time attention, and they wouldn't be trying to put me on lock. Plus, married men would pay to play.

Sex was a powerful drug in my life. I would sex married men like crazy, then gladly send them on their way to their unsuspecting wives, many of whom believed they had a wonderful, faithful, loving husband.

My goal was never to hurt the wife, I was just on a selfish rampage. The men were good for two temporary things; sex and money. Every now and then, I'd get one who got the game twisted and assumed he could tell me what I could and could not do. Those confused married men were released to return to their wives because there was no way a married man had any power over me. Everything about a man that was worth dealing with was in the bottom half of his body, and his best assets were his wallet.

During this time in my life, I partied a lot because the attention I received was insane. It was all about trying to fill the void I felt and that led me to many places and introduced me to many frenemies. One of them, Tamiko, I thought was going to be a real friend. I couldn't have been more wrong.

Tamiko was a former exotic dancer with a body to admire and a personality that truly stood out. She was almost a reflection of me. Her carelessness for life, her nature to use men with money, and the love she had for money mirrored everything I was going through.

Tamiko and I hung out, clubbed, and chilled together. We even let our kids hang together.

One day when I was over at her house, she dropped a bombshell that would set my life on a different course.

"Marisa, I'm about to get paid. Fifteen grand to be exact," she said.

That made me sit up. I definitely wanted to know what kind of come-up she had that would bring in that kind of money.

"It's easy. My boy has this thing going-"

"You don't want to mess with no drugs," I quickly told her.

"Girl, this has nothing to do with slanging. This is quick and easy, and you should get in, too."

My mind immediately started thinking of what I could do with fifteen grand. "Okay, I'm listening."

Tamiko proceeded to fill me in. "You'll open up a bank account and a guy working inside the bank will make the deposit for you, the amount will be $15-thousand. The only catch is that you have to pay him $2,000 once you get the money out."

That sounded too good. "Okay, so how do we get the money out?"

She grinned like she was letting me in on a major secret. "You go to ATM machines, but most of it you'll have to get out through the branches. You'll have to make sure you're dressed professionally so you won't look suspect. You have to get all the money out within twenty-four hours once the check clears. The banks won't see the withdrawals until later that day. So go to a variety of different banks," she explained.

I thought about her words. "And why are you sharing this with me?" I asked.

"Because you're my girl, number one. And number two, there're only so many banks I can cover." She shrugged. "But if you don't want in, I can find someone else who may want this cash."

"Nah, I didn't say that," I quickly interjected. "I'm definitely interested."

It sounded simple enough and having to give that guy $2,000 wasn't much out of the $15,000 that I would get. The next morning, I was at the bank, nervous as all get out. But I was dressed like I was on my way to work. I smiled as I told the woman, "I'd like to open an account."

"Of course, I'd be happy to help you."

It took less than ten minutes for me to open the account. I was unsure if this whole thing would work, but I followed Tamiko's instructions and waited a few days for the check to clear. My stomach was in knots as I called the bank on that third day. I went through the prompts to check my balance.

"Your checking account has an available balance of $15,025.00."

I almost fell out of my seat when the automated system gave me the news. I jumped up and got ready to start hitting the banks one after the other. I made sure I was dressed to impress because I wanted to make sure they didn't look at me too crazy.

First, I hit an ATM. When that fresh cash came gliding into my hand from the machine, I wanted to do a backflip.

"Oh yes, it's on!" I muttered. I hustled the whole day, going between ATMs (until that was maxed out) and going into bank branches. When I was done, I was ready to play.

I stopped by Tamiko's house. As soon as I handed her the $2,000, she smiled at me. "See, I told you it was easy."

"It sure was," I replied.

"You're gonna get hooked," she laughed.

"I already am," I replied before I went on my way.

Chapter 29

During this time, I reconnected with a former boyfriend. Mark was always a character and kept me laughing. He wasn't looking for anything serious and neither was I. We both just wanted to have fun. We often went to the pool hall, out to eat, hung out at his brother's house, and even went to the club together. He was that boy, my homie, lover, friend. It wasn't complicated, it was just fun. He smoked cigarettes just like me, but he also drank, and definitely smoked weed. One night he convinced me to smoke weed with him, something I had never done and regret to this day. "C'mon Marisa you'll be fine" I looked at him with the I don't trust you like that look, but my dumbass did it anyway. I was so high I could barely see, till this day I wonder was it weed or crack because I was certifiably fucked up. I felt super sexy, but super crazy, it got so bad I couldn't even see good enough to drive myself home so I had to trust the drunk Mark to drive. I survived that night, and many nights having fun with him minus the weed activity. But somewhere along the line, Mark became needy. It was probably because he didn't have his own car, he lived with his brother, and he was always around me. Because of the amount of time we spent together, we both ended up falling in love – something I definitely didn't want to happen. No longer was Mark just a piece of my life - he was a part of my life.

Before Mark and I got together, he was talking to another woman and surprisingly, she found out she was pregnant right when he and I realized that we wanted to be in a relationship. At that point I should have pressed the gas and hauled ass out of dodge, but Mark begged me to stay.

"Please, Marisa, I can't go through this without you. I need you, please don't leave me," he cried.

I thought about it and let my emotions overrule my common sense and committed myself to bullshit. To make the situation more crazy, Mark told me his ex wanted an abortion and conveniently I had the $200 that was needed to get rid of the woman. I never had a heart for abortion, but I was in a selfish, self-centered, and heartless phase in my life that led me to do a lot of awful, thoughtless things. Fortunately, she didn't get the abortion and I was happy because the guilt would have eventually caught my heart and squeezed it.

Oddly though, Mark never gave me the money back after she'd made the decision to keep the baby. I didn't trip on it, though, because I still had some money.

But two weeks later, when I went to check my balance, I was floored when the automated teller said, "Your balance is $327.54."

Just two weeks before, I had $13,000. How in the world had I run through that in two weeks? I hadn't paid my car note or rent. I did pay the light and cell phone bills, and constantly put gas in my car. But the rest of the money I'd spent frivolously, especially at the strip club, where I had shelled out hundreds on my favorite male exotic dancer. Then there was the fair, where I balled out of control, and of course, I shopped.

So much money gone so quickly and right then, my life began falling apart. I found out I was pregnant, then, my car was repossessed, and I got an eviction notice.

What was happening to me? I had no directions for my life, and I had no idea how I was going to fix the catastrophe in my life. I decided I needed to start working, but before I could even begin the job search, I started bleeding and my doctor took me off work. She told me not to even lift a gallon of milk.

My pregnancy was at risk, so there was no way I could go out and make money. Mark was working, but he was as irresponsible as I was.

This should have been an easier time. Not only because I'd made all that money with Tamiko, but my twin sister, her boyfriend, Mark and I all lived in the same house. We should have all been contributing. But we were all irresponsible and no one knew what to do about it.

The way we all came under one roof happened before any of us could even blink an eye. Like I told you, when I left my ex-husband, I first went to live with my mom, but her rules were so strict and I was grown. Too grown. And my mother wasn't having it. My sister was living there too, and our mother ended up putting both of us out – I mean, she really put us out -- threw our stuff on the doorstep out.

At the time, I was furious; I couldn't believe she would do this to her own children. But, we consistently failed to follow her rules, and looking back, she did what she needed to do. Even though we weren't raised that way, my sister and I had become disrespectful, we came in the house all times of the night and all times of the morning. We were just downright rude.

The night our mother put our stuff out, was one of the worst nights of our adult relationship.

Alisha and I came in around midnight and she was the first to notice our stuff on the porch.

"Umm, what is this?"

I had been turning it up, and partying, so it took a minute for me to focus.

"Is that my shit?" I said when Alisha held up one of my jackets.

"It's all of our stuff," my sister said as she started sifting through the pile of clothes, CDs, and other personal items.

"What the. . . ?" I immediately went to unlock the front door. The bottom lock turned, but the deadbolt was on, so the door didn't budge.

"Did she put us out?" Alisha asked.

I started banging on the door. "Awww hell, naw! Mama! Mama!" I screamed.

We didn't care that it was late. We both just started banging. And banging. And banging.

My mother never came to the door, and my fury grew. Even with the deadbolt, I knew we didn't have the sturdiest of doors, so I kicked, and hit, and kicked and hit, and kicked and hit until it gave way.

Alisha grabbed my phone and immediately called my mother because she wasn't home. It took us a moment to remember that she was out celebrating my grandparents' anniversary.

"Did you put us out?" Alisha asked, the moment my mother answered our call..

"I'm tired," my mother stated. "I don't know where I went wrong, but I'm tired of both of you. You're disrespectful, headed down the wrong path, and I refuse to let you bring me down with you!"

"What the hell ever," Alisha said. "Just let us get the rest of our shit and you don't ever have to see us again."

We ignored my mother's sobs as we hung up and I kicked the door one more good time. "I'm getting my shit."

Alisha looked at me with amazement in her eyes. "Marisa, what tha hell."

"She's putting us out on the streets," I continued in my rage.

Of course, as Alisha and I raged, all of the kids started crying. We got the rest of our stuff and left. And as the sun rose, we moved into a nearby motel with no idea of what the future held. We were officially homeless with our kids. I was so angry, lost, and resentful toward everyone. I truly couldn't understand what I had done to my mother because I was lost in my world and in my emotions. My mom didn't deserve the treatment she received, she was always such a good role model for us but we took her for granted. We tricked ourselves to believe that she owed us something. Entitlement is a serious mind game because we quickly learned that if someone wants to do something for you it's because they want to, not because they have to. Our mom owed us nothing, she had given us all of her and it was time for her to live for her.

"You think we should apologize to Mama and ask to come back home?" Alisha asked after we'd been in the motel for three days.

"Hell, naw. The last thing I want to do is go groveling back to her. And it's just gonna piss me off more if she says no. We just have to make it work."

And make it work we did. We took odd jobs; one night Alisha would work, and the next night, I would work. We made barely enough to pay for the small motel room. But we tagged team as much as possible to make ends meet. It still wasn't enough, though, because we eventually had to stay in a shelter.

That became our cycle. We'd go to a shelter, but keep working and save enough money for a few more nights in a motel. Then, when that money ran out, we'd return to the shelter.

It was a revolving door. Alisha's boyfriend, Jonathan, would come to visit sometimes, which would have been good if he actually would have brought something to the table, but he only added to the struggle.

After getting a full time job at a dialysis center, eventually, I found a house that we could afford. It was $650.00 a month. We moved in and Jonathan moved right in with us, then Mark came to live with us, too. We were all back together, but we were doing the same thing. We were a group of irresponsible young adults all under one roof, making a mess of life.

Mark and Jonathan constantly drank and smoked weed and all my sister and I did was hang out and spend what little money we managed to bring in.

Chapter 30

The irresponsible life caught up with us. We received an eviction notice. We had ten days to vacate our house or the sheriff's deputy was going to put us out.

One day, Mark and I were at his brother, Sam's house, kicking back, doing nothing. Sam was a pretty smart guy, soft-spoken, and about ten years older than us. We'd just told him about our financial situation and he smiled.

"I think I might have something to help you out of your bind," he said. Sam started telling us about what he was doing and my antenna flew up.

"My girl, Tamiko, had me in on that."

Sam shook his head. "Naw, this is a little different. This is a lot more money, and a lot more hands on. You will have to get two accounts open. One will be for you to deposit the checks I give you into them, the next one will be for you to get paid, and give me my cut."

His eyes immediately went to my belly.

"Yo, I don't know, Ma, with you being pregnant and all."

"I can do this," I said. "I need money and I need it quick." I rubbed my stomach. "If anything, my baby will work in my favor. Who will suspect a pregnant woman?"

My life was steadily falling to pieces. So what better way to fix it than with the one thing I needed most, money?

"There's a lot of money involved," Sam said. He looked like he was thinking for a minute, then he added, "But I guess all you're really doing is opening the accounts and making deposits."

It still sounded pretty simple and foolproof because deposits were fast and easy if you had the correct information. And considering you could make a deposit into anyone's account, it wouldn't be complicated.

I was ecstatic. My life was about to change!

Whoever said money couldn't buy happiness had obviously never been broke.

I was on a money high. I was happy with money, I needed no one when I had money, and people adored me when I had money.

Sam started off with small checks that gave me some quick money. This was only a couple of hundred dollars at a time but this bought me a little time on the house and our shit wasn't thrown into the street. I was ready for the big money, because I knew I could buy everything I needed for my unborn baby. On top of that I was flossing, and it felt good all over again. My sister saw my hair, all my new clothes, all the joy I had, and how my life was changing. The curiosity was all over her face, and one day she asked me, "Whatever it is that you're doing to get all this cash, you haven't gotten caught?"

I flashed a wicked smile. "Nope."

She looked like she was weighing her words. "I want some money, too. I'm tired of struggling."

Of course, I completely understood where she was coming from. After making sure that she was serious, I set up a meeting with Sam, who reluctantly agreed to bring her in.

Mark really didn't care about me running the check scam, but Jonathan hit the roof, which was crazy to me since his trifling behind wasn't bringing in any money. When he did bring in money, he kept it to himself.

I think Alisha was getting tired of Jonathan and his negativity anyway, so his words were worthless in our ears. We were determined and ready to get the money so we could have a better life for us and our kids. Now it was time to play in the big leagues and we were game!

Chapter 31

We met Sam at a local restaurant to discuss details. He'd found someone to open the account that was needed to make the deposits. Alisha and I opened an account for the transfer to be made once the deposits were made.

Sam gave us a stack of checks inside of an envelope. The checks were already signed and ready for the drop. Some checks were for $10,000 and others were for $15,000. We were excited and confident that this would no doubt change our lives. The plan was simple; go through the drive-thru, make the deposit, and leave.

We made it to the first bank and it was easy as one-two-three. Then, we arrived at the second bank. Alisha was driving her black Chevrolet Beretta as we pulled up to the drive-thru teller. Everything was going as planned until the teller asked Alisha to give her an ID for the deposit. Instantly, red flags went up everywhere in my mind. They never asked for IDs for deposits.

"Alisha, do not give them your ID," I hissed.

She turned to me and whispered, "I don't have a choice. They have my face on camera. I can't just take off."

I knew she was right, but still I knew that something wasn't right. No matter how much I insisted, she gave her ID to them anyway. My heart was racing and paranoia set in; I knew something was wrong.

My suspicions were confirmed when the teller said, "We need you to come inside to get your IDD."

My eyes bucked. "No! Do not go in. We need to drive off now!"

"They don't have your ID. They have mine!"

What the fuck was happening?

My panic went into overdrive as my sister pulled around to the front of the building and parked.

"I'll be back," she said as she got out of the car.

"Please, hurry." I looked around the parking lot. Everything looked normal, but my nerves were completely on edge.

I sat in the car with the kids, who we'd brought along because this was supposed to be a drive-thru event only, not a sit and stay or mix and mingle.

After a few minutes, the kids started getting antsy. Shantel was only three years old. Rashard was two, and Ramon was one. The anxiety continued to build as I looked around, checking out my surroundings.

Finally, I decided to get out. "I'm going to be right back so stay right here," I told the kids before running into the bank. I was four months pregnant with my second daughter and it was obvious that I was carrying a small load when I walked into the bank.

I cased the building and noticed Alisha sitting at a desk to the left, talking to a black woman as though she knew her.

What the hell? was my only thought as I walked over.

"Hey, Alisha, we need to go. The kids are getting fussy, it's time for their lunch."

Alisha looked up at me, her eyes filled with sadness. "Girl, this lady just lost her daughter who was only twenty-one years old."

That lady had lost her daughter, but my sister had lost her damn mind. Was she really sitting here chit-chatting with this woman? "Oh, that's horrible, sorry to hear that," I quickly said, "but Alisha, the kids. . ."

We were interrupted by her desk phone ringing. I held my breath as she picked up the phone, hesitated, then said, "The checks cleared?"

Alisha seemed a little relieved, but my shit-is-about-to-blow-up radar was on full blast. We didn't need for the checks to clear. We just needed to make a deposit. This didn't even sound right.

145

"Alisha. . ." I mumbled.

But before we could say another word, an officer walked through the door. Instinctively, our eyes were to the white man with jet-black hair.

"Are they still here?" he asked someone standing by the door. When that person pointed toward us, my heart dropped into my ankles.

It felt like the cop was walking in slow motion as he headed our way. I mentally prepared myself to break into a mad dash, but my body was frozen in place.

"Guess you know you two are in big trouble," he said.

Neither of us could say a word. He shook his head as he looked at the black lady, who'd just conned Alisha with her daughter-dying story. "Do they know they could serve ten years in prison for each check?"

The woman didn't reply as she looked at us with disgust.

My voice suddenly found its way back. "Sir, I'm not sure what you're talking about, but our kids are in the car."

"You should've thought about that before you brought them along on your crime spree," he said.

I was shaking now. "Can I at least get them out?" I don't know if I planned to get them, or jump in the car and take off.

"No, I will get them out." I hadn't even noticed the other officer who had walked up behind us.

Think, think, think, Marisa...... What could I say to get myself out of this mess? I wanted to scream. My mind was blank, yet scattered at the same time.

Then, Alisha just busted out crying. "I shouldn't have done it! I shouldn't have done it!" she cried.

Are you fucking kidding me? I wanted to scream. If there was ever a such thing as twin telepathy, I was trying to send it to her now and tell her to shut the hell up.

The officer who had gone to retrieve our kids, reappeared. All of the kids looked really confused, especially once they saw the tears in Alisha's and my eyes. Seeing our kids standing there, I knew that we had to try and pull it together.

The officers took us to the back of the bank, put us in a room and left out. This gave us an opportunity to talk.

"I'm telling," Alisha immediately said.

"Alisha, you can't," I warned. "You can lie."

She violently shook her head. "No, I can't and I won't."

I pounded the table in front of us. "You have to or else this is going to cause major problems for me and Mark. Sam trusted me with this."

I could tell at that point no matter what I said, my sister wasn't trying to hear it. "We're the ones about to go to jail! I'm telling everything! You know if it was you they'd sell you out," she said.

The sad part was, she was right. Both Mark and Sam wouldn't hesitate to kick me under the bus.

"Mommy, what's going on?" my daughter asked me. All I could do was take her into my arms.

We both held our kids and began to cry. After a few minutes, the officers came back in. They were accompanied by two other men, who were dressed in black suits.

"We're with the Secret Service," the first man told us as he slid into a seat across from us. "Do you have anyone you can call to come get your kids because you're going to jail today?"

My heart dropped and we both began to cry, which made the kids cry even harder.

Seeing our babies crying made both of us try to compose ourselves. Alisha and I exchanged glances. We both knew that the only person we could call was our mom.

Hesitantly, I grabbed the phone and dialed her number. I only prayed she answered. I was grateful when she did.

"Hey, Mom," I said as I took a deep breath. "Ummmmm, Alisha and I need you to come get the kids."

"Why? You know I'm at work," she replied.

"We got into some trouble and we're at the bank down the

street from your school," I said.

Momentary silence filled the phone. "What did y'all do?" she finally asked.

"Some stuff with some checks and the police are here," I admitted. The officers were sitting there staring at us. Alisha had already admitted our involvement, so there was no use trying to act innocent.

"Both of y'all?" my mother said.

"Can you just come now?"

She took a deep breath. "Okay, but you know my car is messed up, so I have to get someone else to bring me." She hesitated. "Whatever it is you did, couldn't one of you tell the other one not to do it?"

My mom was right, why couldn't one of us tell the other not to do it? We'd been that way most of our lives. But over this past year, it was if we were two lost souls wandering down a dark road to the land of the unknown.

My mother was dropped off, but before she could leave with the kids, the officers told us, "Your mother can take the car, but we have to search it first."

This made things so much worse because all the checks were in the car. But my mom had no other way to take the kids, so we had no choice but to agree.

While they searched the car, the Secret Service questioned us.

"We know you two aren't the masterminds behind this. So we need you to tell us who is," the first agent said.

I spoke up before Alisha started rambling. "We were only asked to drop these off because our friend is at work." I knew the lie sucked, but what could I say? I wasn't ready to tell the whole truth yet. I was still recovering from the shock of getting caught. It was such a shock to me because of all the other times when I'd done it before Alisha. I'd never been caught.

The agent rolled his eyes at me and turned to Alisha. "Is that your story, too?"

Alisha, surprisingly, was cautious with her words, but she tried to comply with the Secret Service. It was obvious we were not on the same page.

After about fifteen minutes of back and forth, an officer stuck his head in the door.

"The car's been searched. We have what we need," he said.

The Secret Service agents got up and walked out. That once again left us with the opportunity to talk. Only, we didn't know what else to say. Our tears came again, but this time, Alisha took it a step further and started speaking in tongues. All I could think was, *I've done it. I've really messed up.*

Two officers came back in, as well as more Secret Service agents. There were so many law enforcement agents there that it looked like we had robbed the bank at gunpoint.

Finally, the first two Secret Service agents came back in, and with a straight face one of them said, "Take them to jail."

"Noooooooo!" I cried. This could not be happening. This could not be real!

If there was any glimmer to be found in that tragic day, it was the officer who walked over to take us into custody.

"We will not handcuff you two in front of your kids," he whispered. "We do not want them to see you that way."

"Thank you," we both managed to mumble.

We walked from the back with our kids, and saw our mom standing there. Disappointment blanketed her face. It was so hard and heavy on my heart because I was so wrong. The kids didn't know or understand anything, but they could feel enough to be upset. I felt so low and horrible for what I'd done to my mother, my kids and myself.

The officers separated us. Alisha was led to one police car and I went to another.

Outside, the officer told me, "Turn around and put your hands behind your back."

I complied, and felt so embarrassed and stupid as he began to read me my rights. Then, he opened the door to the police car and put me in the back. Because I was so embarrassed, I laid down in the back of the police car the entire ride over to the station.

We arrived at the police station at the same time, after what seemed like forever, the 15 minute drive finally came to an end and I could get my butt off that hard seat. We were booked, stripped searched, and told to bend over, spread our cheeks and cough. It was such a degrading and humiliating experience.

They eventually put both my sister and I in separate rooms and that's when the real interrogation began. It was one question after the next. Who, what, when, where and why? I felt like they were drilling my brain, the way a carpenter drilled a floor when putting in hardwood floors. I tried to lie, but it was like they knew every lie from every truth. Had they been watching us the whole time? Or could they really be that good?

Out of nowhere, they switched on us and my agent went in to interrogate Alisha and hers came to interrogate me. They started using our stories against us. Alisha spared no details, which instantly put a chokehold on any lies I intended to tell. Then the threats of prison time got dropped on the table and shit got real. They brought up the kids, my pregnancy and ultimately, all my bravado went out the window. They broke me down.

I knew that by now, Mark and Jonathan were wondering where we were. We had been gone since earlier that day and they hadn't seen or heard from us.

I had no idea how or why, but after hours and hours of interrogation, an agent came into the room where they'd been grilling me.

"We're gonna let you ladies go home tonight. You just have to promise to come to our office in the morning," the agent said. I didn't ask any questions. I just immediately agreed to return.

I was feeling so lost and ashamed when I called my mom. Although our mom was disappointed, she said that she would come to get us. And we both waited outside, looking like two lost souls.

Chapter 32

The longest day of my life turned into the longest night. Mark immediately lit into me when I walked in the house.

"Where the hell have you been?"

"Jail," I said, falling back on the sofa, exhausted. I would've given anything not to have this conversation right now, but I knew I wouldn't get off that easy. Alisha and Jonathan had already retreated to their bedroom where I was sure she was spilling everything.

I started at the beginning and didn't stop until I was at our being released. Mark stood wide-eyed and in shock the entire time. But I was the one who was shocked when instead of asking how I was doing, Mark said, "Tell me you did not tell on Sam? You know he been down this road before, and he got a son!"

All I could think to say was, "Really? I have a four-year-old and I'm pregnant with your child and all you can think about is your brother?"

He continued to fuss and act the fool until I told him, "Mark, I'm tired. I'm looking at prison time. Do you know that they found over $260,000 worth of checks in the car? It wasn't just the police. It was Secret Service. THE FEDS and I don't have time to be listening to this bullshit right now. I'm worried about what's going to happen to me!"

That shut him up, thank goodness, and I was able to try to gather my thoughts and prepare for the next day.

The next morning, as promised, Alisha and I went down to Secret Service. We went, but we weren't prepared.

They took us into a back room, sat us down, and there it was - my past ready to slap me in the face. All across the table were pictures of me at various banks.

This cannot be happening, I thought as I stared at the pictures.

The Secret Service agent was calm as he said, "Do you know what these are?"

"Pictures of me?" I don't know why I said that as a question instead of a statement. There was no denying that was me. They had pictures of me, Tamiko, her boyfriend, Sam, and even a few extra people I didn't know. All of the banks I thought I'd gotten away with were sitting right here front and center.

The agents once again came in hard with the questions. I gave up. I wasn't even going to try and lie my way out of anything anymore. Maybe if I was honest, they'd have some kind of mercy on me.

I told as much as I knew, but the thing was, I'd been lied to, so what I was saying was all a lie. Tamiko had run game on me because there was no middleman. That $2,000 fee I'd paid back when I'd done this with her, she pocketed. I was pissed to say the least.

They proceeded to ask more questions about Sam, and then they went back and asked more about Tamiko. It was like a tennis match going back and forth. By the time I left, I was so confused about my future because now I had two felonies looming in front of me.

Just a few days later, the Feds raided Sam's house. He was arrested and then bailed out within a week. Mark didn't hesitate to let me know how furious he was. But at that point, Mark and Sam were the least of all the concerns I had.

I guess the hardest part in all of this chaos was accepting that I did this to myself. I wasn't ready for that truth. I blamed everything else: my circumstances, my pregnancy, even my ex-husband. For me, like with so many people, it was always easier to look at an outside source to my inside mess-ups. I couldn't run from me and my responsibility any longer.

Alisha and I were subpoenaed to court within a month to be arraigned. Although neither one of us wanted a court-appointed lawyer, we didn't have any other choice because we spoke to a few attorneys and the minimum they would accept to even start the case was $6,000. Of course that made me feel like I was in as deep as the Grand Canyon. Things were not looking up for us.

During the arraignment, a lot happened that sent my world into a tailspin. But I found comfort in the fact that it could have been worse. Unfortunately for Sam, he was taken back into custody that day. The prosecutor had no mercy and to make matters worse Sam, received the same judge who had sent him to prison the last time.

"Didn't I tell you that I didn't want to see you back in my court-room?" the judge asked Sam.

"Yes," Sam mumbled.

She shook her head in disgust. "Bailiff take him into custody."

No sooner had they scuttled Sam out of the room, then the prosecutor turned his fury on us.

"Your honor, I would also recommend that Marisa Readus and Alisha Readus be taken into custody as well. They have a history of violent behavior throughout school," he said.

I looked at him in amazement. Was he really going back to high school? That was years before. My heart beat with anticipation as the judge looked at us.

After a brief hesitation, the judge said, "I will not be placing the Readus sisters into custody, but they will be placed on proba-tion until sentencing."

That brought on a big sigh of relief from the both of us. But our relief was short-lived when the judge ran down our charges.

"Marisa Readus, you are being charged with bank fraud, con-spiracy, and attempt to defraud the bank. You currently have two felonies that you are being charged with. Do you understand the charges?"

"Yes," I replied.

"Alisha Readus, you are being charged with attempt to defraud the bank and conspiracy. Do you understand that you are being charged with one felony?"

"Yes, I understand," my sister said.

Finally, court adjourned and we were appointed attorneys, who proceeded to explain that we were facing one to five years in prison.

That information was a total shock because I didn't even get money the second time around and Alisha didn't get any money at all.

The probation officer also came over and ran down all the strict guidelines we were to follow while we waited to be sentenced. There was a lot of paperwork and a lot to think about. Between the probation officers and the attorneys, there was all kind of legal lingo being tossed around. Words like "plea bargain," "restricted access," and "limited travel" peppered the air.

What was life going to be like? I was never a person with so many boundaries and limitations. I always played by my own rules, but now the game was changing. And I had more questions than ever. Do I plead guilty or not guilty? Go to trial or take the plea bargain. It was overwhelming facing so much, and preparing to lose even more.

Chapter 33

My life was being torn to pieces. I needed help. I needed grace. I needed peace, but more than anything I needed a savior. I found that in March of 1999. That's the day I was born again and submitted my whole life with my whole heart to Christ.

I had been running from the call because I didn't want to be a hypocrite, and I didn't want to fail.

But at this point in my life, I realized that I couldn't fix me, and that God had something to give that I was missing. He accepted me the way I was - broken, empty, sad, hurt, lonely, and hungry for change. God loved me no matter what, and He knew my end from my beginning. God designed me for greatness even though I couldn't see it or feel it at the time. I had to trust in what I didn't see because everything else in my life that I could see was a mess. Faith was all I had.

After giving my life to Christ, I truly wanted change in my life. Yes, I was shacking up, pregnant, and still legally married to another man, but my heart was in the right place and Mark hated it. He couldn't understand my determination and the peace that I longed for. We argued more and the stress was overwhelming for the both of us, and we did not see eye to eye. I became more and more dependent on Mark as my pregnancy progressed and he couldn't handle it. Night after night, he stayed out drinking and smoking weed.

One night as I was laying in the bed, Mark came in and slammed the door. Instantly, I jumped up and I saw him walk in the room with my daughter, Shantel's, car seat.

"Man, I got stopped by the police," he snapped.

"Okay."

"Your car got impounded during a road block."

I blinked twice, trying to process what he was saying. "Wait, hold up. Did you just say my car got impounded?"

"Yeah, I'm lucky they didn't take me to jail because I don't have a license."

My first instinct was to go clean off. But I tried to remain calm. "So how are we going to get my car back, Mark?"

"I get paid Friday so don't start tripping!"

I sighed. "Mark, I have a doctor's appointment Friday at eleven in the morning so we need to get it first thing in the morning."

"We will. Damn that was close."

I was so disgusted with his stupidity, I just decided to get back in the bed and go to sleep.

Friday came and Mark decided he wanted to play hardball. He came through the door and the chaos began.

I was sitting in the living room waiting for my sister. "Hey, Mark, Alisha is on her way to get me so I need the money to get the car out of impound," I told him.

"Oh, I don't have it," he said like it was no big deal.

I paused, looked down, glanced up, and stepped up right in his face.

"Look here, you 'bout to give up that money one way or another or it's about to go down in this bitch!" I knocked the coffee table over, pissed to the highest level of pisstivity.

"You'd better not hit me, Marisa."

"Your ass better cough up that money!"

"I ain't doing shit, bitch!"

I stepped up closer to him, with a closed fist ready to knock him out for getting my car impounded in the first place. I'd never been afraid of a fight and pregnant or not, it was about to go down. I guess he figured I wasn't about to back down because he began digging in his pocket and handed me the money. I looked him up and down and walked out.

My relationship with Mark was getting worse by the day. After that one Saturday a few weeks later, he came to me and asked if he could use my car although he still didn't have a license.

I politely replied, "No." I was tired of all of his hanging out that led to problems at home like our disconnected utilities. I had no way of communicating with anyone outside of our home and I was hungry all the time, not to mention that I was about to be sent to prison. My life was in shambles, and Mark was worried about going out in my car.

Of course, he got upset when I told him he couldn't have my car.

"See, this is that bull. Give me the damn keys."

"I said no," I said, keeping my voice steady and determined.

"Man. . ." He reached for the keys on the dresser. I grabbed a fan that was also sitting on the dresser and slammed it across his face. We started fighting and I held my own, blow for blow, until he picked me up and threw me on the bed. Before I could bounce up, he closed his hands around my neck and he started choking me.

There was no way I was going out like that. As I fought to get air, I reached out and managed to grab the iron sitting on the nightstand. I swung it, barely missing his face. He dove out of the way, giving me time to push him off of me. I scrambled out of the room, snatched up my daughter, and got the hell out of the house.

Mark was always drinking, always smoking weed, and always blaming me for his horrible habits and addictions, which was crazy because he was doing all of this stuff before I even met him. Once again I was with a man who blamed me for everything that was wrong in his world.

My sister was the only person I could call. No matter what was going on, she was always caring and there to listen to me without judgment. Alisha was staying with some lady from church named Melva, she wasn't living alone. But I didn't know where else to turn.

Fortunately, I was able to spend the night over there and it was the break I needed. But her space was cramped and after a couple of days, I knew I couldn't stay.

I didn't want to go to a shelter and couldn't go back and live with my mom, so I did the only thing I could do – I went back to Mark.

But returning to Mark, opened a new door of horrible in our relationship.

Mark was fine with me coming back, but then one night, Mark's friend was having a party and I tagged along, leaving my daughter with a neighbor. Boy, do I wish I would have stayed home, but a lot of things became clear to me that night.

I was outside mingling with people by the pool. Hours went by and eventually I was ready to go. But when I went to search for Mark, he had disappeared. I went upstairs and found him in the back room with some of his friends.

"Hey, Mark," I said, approaching him. "I'm tired, so I'm about to leave. Can someone bring you home?" I stopped suddenly when I saw what he and his friends were doing. When I saw the white stuff around his nose.

"Is-is that cocaine?" I asked.

He quickly wiped his nose. "Wh-?"

When his boys started laughing, I knew that it was.

"Are you freakin' kidding me?" I screamed.

Mark tried to act casual. "So? I snort cocaine. It ain't nothing." He laughed as he dapped his boys. "It's all good, Marisa."

"Oh, naw the hell it ain't!" I screamed. "You're one step away from being a crackhead. Now I see why we've been sitting in the apartment, in the dark, and don't have nothing because you're a fuckin' junkie!"

I walked away crying and so upset that I was pregnant by this man. How would my child be affected by someone who had alcohol and drug problems? I had a prison sentence looming over me and I was supposed to rest easy knowing my daughter was with someone like that?

As I drove home, I kept imagining him selling my child for

drugs.

My mind was running all over the place as I tearfully drove. Once again I was afraid, afraid for my baby, afraid for me, and afraid that I would continue to mess up. I kept bringing these dysfunctional men into my life. I was determined to break that cycle, though. I needed to figure out how to get away from Mark.

I knew I couldn't go where my sister was staying, so I decided to call a domestic violence hotline. I'd been keeping a phone number in my wallet for months.

As tears ran down my face, I stood in the phone booth and punched in the number.

"Hi, may I help you?" the woman answered.

"Yes, please. I need help." I burst into tears before I could finish talking.

"Okay, calm down. Are you currently in danger?"

I took a deep breath and tried to compose myself. The weight of everything was just bearing down on me.

"No, not immediately. But there has been violence and I'm seven months pregnant and have a four-year-old daughter. I. . . I . . . I don't know what to do."

She proceeded to ask me questions and as she spoke, her voice was kind and understanding, which put my heart at ease and calmed me down. She gave me all the information I needed to make a smooth transition. Fortunately, while I was at the phone booth, I saw a police officer. I figured Mark had made it home by now, so I asked the officer to come with me. All I wanted to do was get my things and I didn't have the energy for any more fights; I just wanted to leave.

When I walked into the house, Mark eyeballed me as the police stood by.

"What's going on, Marisa?" he asked.

The officer took a step forward. "Sir, she is just here to get her things and leave peacefully."

Mark glared at me and grunted. But I didn't care. I just wanted something different. I wanted to pack me and my daughter's things, go pick her up from the sitter, and figure out the rest of my life.

Hours later, I arrived at the shelter with my daughter in tow. I was glad to see that it was newly renovated and the staff was caring. Right now, I needed someone to care and understand me without judgment. The lady who helped me, Kim, was a wonderful, sweet woman with a kind heart. She cared about what I was going through and helped me fill out all the paperwork. When I was done, they took me to my room. There were two twin beds, two dressers, and a bathroom. The beds were really comfortable and I was happy when I was able to lay down and finally rest without having to argue, worry about an argument, or being awakened by the smell of alcohol-filled breath.

Over the next few days, I heard that Mark was asking everyone where I was and begging for people to get a message to me to call him. But, I was focused on trying to create a future without him.

During my stay in the shelter, I applied for transitional housing, which is an apartment, but dirt-cheap with all utilities and expenses included in the rent. Unfortunately, there was a waiting list, so I could not move in immediately. I was okay with that because the maximum time to stay at the shelter was three months and I was hopeful that the apartment would come available right around that time. The shelter provided great resources and daycare so Shantel was able to stay there while I ran errands and went to the doctor.

One day, I needed someone to pick me up because I had no gas and, I could not walk very far. So I called a friend and gave her the address where I was staying.. I had no idea that she would call me back afterward and ask to speak to me, telling the director that besides the address that I'd given her, she needed directions.

The shelter was in an undisclosed location and apparently, me giving out the address was a huge violation.

Even though I wasn't aware that I'd broken a major rule, and even though I wept profusely, and was truly sorry, the shelter had to put me out.

Once again, I had nowhere to go. I found some information on a homeless shelter and I called there and spoke with an older white woman. Her voice was sweet and full of energy and she helped me feel a little better about the change I was having to make.

After I spoke with her, I gathered all of my belongings, went to the shelter and met with the woman I'd spoken to. When I walked in there and saw the homeless people in the kitchen eating, I looked around, thinking, *I don't want to be like these people. I don't want to be homeless.*

I felt so sad as I sat with Shantel and ate. Some people were obviously suffering from drug abuse, others, mental illness, and then there were those like me who were just homeless. I didn't want Shantel in that environment, so once I was taken to my room, I went into the sitting area and called my friend, Carol.

"Can you do me a huge favor?" I asked.

"What do you need?"

"Can I bring Shantel over to you tomorrow?" That's all I said; I didn't feel like going into the specifics of what was going on, and with my friend, I didn't have to.

All Carol said was, "Yes."

At that time, Carol had four children of her own, and I knew she was a great mother who was gentle, patient, and understanding. So there was no one better than her. I didn't ask to stay with her because her husband didn't like me and anyway, I was concerned more about Shantel's safety more than anything else.

Back inside my room, I stood for a moment and stared at the two sets of bunk beds. They were really small beds and I knew it would be hard to squeeze my pregnant self between those beds. I put Shantel on the bunk above me, then got into the lower bed. There was another girl in the room, who obviously didn't like the intrusion. But as uncomfortable as I was with the bed and our roommate, I fell asleep grateful that at least I wasn't in my car or on a bench.

I couldn't wait to get out of there the next morning. I made it to Carol's house and expressed my gratitude, but her husband didn't hesitate to tell me that she couldn't stay longer than a week.

"We got too many kids here as it is," he snapped.

That didn't leave me much choice. There was nothing I could do in a week – except figure out how to make things work with Mark. My court date for my sentencing was coming up soon. I needed to give my newborn the only stability I could – and that meant going back to Mark.

Chapter 34

The day arrived for court and boy, was I nervous. This would be the day that I would plead guilty to my crime. My mom came, but my dad was still in Huntsville and we were giving him updates about what was happening. I knew they both were so disappointed in me and Alisha. Thinking about how my dad was a respectable man who worked for the government, and my mom being a business teacher made me even more ashamed.

How did I turn into such a mess? I often wondered and I was wondering that now as I stood next to my sister in the courtroom.

"All Rise!" As the bailiff made his announcement, my heart raced in anticipation. This was happening, it was really happening.

This would be the first time I would take full responsibility for my actions. The date was July 12, 1999, a Thursday. A date I would never forget.

The bailiff brought Sam into the courtroom. When I saw him, my heart sank deep into my gut. He glared at me as one name after the other was called to face the judge. Finally, they got to me.

"Marisa Readus Ross versus The United States Of America," the judge said.

Really? The United States of America? What the hell was that about? Did I do this to the entire United States?

Nevertheless, I stood at attention and listened to the judge tell me my charges once again, and then she asked me the ultimate question, "How do you plead?"

I paused, then said, "Guilty."

Although I wanted to scream my innocence, there was no running from the truth.

I watched the judge's eyes take me in and her glance settled on my stomach. "When are you due?" she asked.

"August 16th," I replied.

She shook her head pitifully. "Okay, we will set the sentencing date for September 16."

I was thankful she took my pregnancy into consideration because that was one of my fears - that either I would be in labor or still recovering from having the baby when I had to report to jail. At least she was giving me a month with my baby.

There were a few other cases including my sister's, and then court adjourned. While I was grateful for the extension for sentencing, the facts hadn't changed. I was looking at one to five years in prison. I didn't want prison at all; I wanted my freedom, my life, my kids, and another chance to get it right. I wanted all of that, even though I wasn't even sure if I would be able to get it right. But I wanted the chance to try.

Still, I was going to prison, so all I could do was prepare for the birth of my baby and then my sentencing. While I tried my best to live a stress-free life over the next two months, I was faced with another bombshell.

Mark had to tell me something that he'd been keeping from me. He had another baby. A baby born in June by the girl he was with before me. When I found that out, my stress went to a whole other level. Not only was I upset that he had this other woman pregnant at the same time that I was, but I was angry because he seemed to be angry. I didn't know what he had to be upset about, but he was. Maybe it was because he had two women pregnant at the same time. Whatever, this situation had come from his own irresponsibility.

But I had to handle it. I had to handle it even when the baby came to visit, which she did one night in August. She was just two months old and I was nine months pregnant. I'd been upset, until I saw that little baby. She was simply beautiful with her light red sandy hair. Everything from that hair to her complexion made her the spitting image of Mark.

I cared for her like she was my own and being with her made me even more excited that I was about to give birth to my own little girl soon. I held that baby and talked to her and enjoyed every moment.

The night she came to stay with us, I had her in the bedroom with me, while Mark was in the living room watching television. She'd fallen asleep and once she was out, I took the opportunity to run some errands.

"I'll be right back," I told Mark. "Running to the store."

"Okay," he grunted.

I was gone less than thirty minutes. When I arrived back home, the house was full of strangers. It took me a moment to look around and find Mark; he was on the balcony smoking weed.

It was difficult for me to put two thoughts together as I rushed to check on Shantel. She was still asleep in her room. I eased the door closed, then headed to our bedroom.

I stopped mid-step when I saw some woman I had never met in my bedroom.

"Oh, the baby woke up," the woman said, looking up as I stepped into the room.

I snatched the baby from her. "Who the hell are you?"

"I'm Z's girlfriend," she said, like I really was supposed to know who Z was.

I didn't even have any more words for her. I pulled the baby to my chest, turned and stormed back into the front room.

"Mark, what the hell?" I shouted. "Who are these people?" .

"Oh, these my homies," he said as casually as if he were telling me the time.

"I've never seen them before and some girl was in the room with the baby."

"It's all good."

"No, it's not Mark," I yelled, not caring that everyone was staring at me. "It's not all good." I spun around and pushed past the woman who had followed me out.

I slammed the door to the bedroom and struggled not to cry. I laid the baby down on the bed, then climbed next to her and let the tears flow.

I was about to go to prison. Is this the environment that my baby would be subjected to while I was away? As I thought about that, all I could do was cry.

I kept my distance from Mark for the next two weeks. Then, on August 11th, I started having contractions. Mark was at work, so I timed the contractions myself. As time passed, the contractions got closer and closer together. I waited as long as I could before I drove to the phone booth to call Mark at work and let him know I needed to go to the hospital. I had to go to the phone booth because our home phone had been cut off.

"It's time," I said, once his supervisor had gotten him on the phone. "The baby is coming."

"What?" he said. "All right. You need to come get me from work, though."

I couldn't believe it. I was having to pick up my man, while I was in labor!

I took small deep breaths as I gripped the steering wheel and drove toward Mark's job. Amazingly, I made it and Mark ran out as soon as I pulled up. He helped me into the passenger seat and then he jumped inside. He was scared to death that I was going to have the baby in the car.

"Mark, calm down. We just need to get to the hospital."

"Shitttt, I've seen these shows."

He drove as if there was no speed limit, as if there were no red lights or stop signs and I was glad that we made it to the hospital. He hopped out of the car, ran inside for the wheelchair and when he pushed me inside, they quickly told us we could go upstairs.

They got me in the observation room and determined I was in active labor and as soon as I hit four centimeters, I told them to get the anesthesiologist for my epidural. My first pregnancy, I tried to pull the Super Woman move and go twenty hours without medication. I'd learned that lesson and was not going without some medically prescribed drugs that could knock those contractions down to size. I wanted them ASAP.

Mark tried to sleep through my intense labor. He'd popped a pill at work, and was just going to sleep through the whole thing, I guess. But that wasn't going to happen. Especially not once I was finally ready to have this baby.

Mark and I were in the room alone and I tossed the cup that the nurse had filled with ice at him while he slept on the small sofa against the wall. When his eyes opened, I screamed, "Go get the nurse! I need to push!"

Luckily for him, the container was empty. He jumped up, ran, got the nurse and for once in his life, he did the right thing. He stayed by my side, holding my hand. And he smiled with me when we heard our baby cry.

My daughter, Asheera, was born at 6:24 a.m. on August 12th. Her cry was so sweet, it brought tears to my eyes.

"She's beautiful. Why are you crying?" Mark asked.

I couldn't form the words I was thinking. My beautiful baby had been brought into my chaotic world. What type of life would she have? Would I have to go to prison and leave her? All kind of thoughts ran through my mind as I looked at her gorgeous face with her headful of thick, black baby doll hair. My bad decisions were about to resonate with my baby.

Just days after having Asheera, my name came up on the transitional housing list. I moved away from Mark as soon as I could pack, and moved into the small apartment that was connected to a homeless shelter. It wasn't much, just a small room with two beds, a kitchen, and a bathroom. Although it had no windows, and the beds slept like box springs, it would work until I had to face my fate.

Chapter 35

I got exactly one month and five days with my baby. Of course, I was praying for a miracle. I wasn't sure what was going to happen during sentencing. My attorney had been scaring the life out of me with every assumption and possibility, all of them worst case scenarios.

And every time I thought things couldn't get worse, they did. Days before my sentencing, I was taking Asheera to the doctor. My oil was low, so I asked my mom for a couple of dollars to get a quart of oil. I picked up Alisha and we headed to our mom's school where she taught.

As we drove, my car suddenly started rumbling, then there was a loud pow sound. Fire emerged from under the car and smoke was everywhere. I managed to make it to the side of the road. We grabbed the kids and ran away from the car and down the highway. People pulled over to see what was happening and someone called the police and fire department.

We had just managed to make it to the side of the road when the car burst into flames. I stood there on the side of the highway crying.

"Why, Lord, why?" I wailed. I knew that I wasn't living my life right, but I didn't understand what I'd done to be punished so.

Now, I really had nothing, and my court date was in two days. What was I going to do? As I stood there thinking and holding my kids, the ambulance arrived. Thank God, we were fine. Physically, I was fine. Mentally and emotionally, I was in shambles.

I could barely function the next two days. My mind was all over the place. For some reason, Proverbs 21 kept running through my mind. I was not a scriptural person (I didn't even know where the Old Testament ended and the New Testament began). I grabbed my Bible and turned to the chapter and began reading.

The King's heart is a stream of water in the hand of the Lord. He turns it wherever He will.

I ended up getting drawn into those words. The entire chapter spoke of unwise decisions, hastiness, and how it could lead to poverty. I closed the Bible, feeling like God had spoken directly to me.

Reading that passage gave me the strength to go to court. It helped me see that I was not alone. Although I didn't know what my future held, I knew God was with me no matter what happened.

The morning of September 16th, I kissed my girls goodbye, then Mark took them to his mom's house while everyone else went to court.

I had on a two-piece suit with heels. I was looking my Sunday Best. The courtroom was filled with my family. Even my grandfather came. Not many words were spoken I don't think anyone knew what to say, but their disappointment was evident.

Court began and I was the first one up.

"Do you have anything to say before I sentence you?" the judge asked.

Instantly, I cried. "I'm sorry, Your Honor. I was wrong. Please have mercy on me. I will never do it again!"

There was no shame in my tears, which were so heavy I could barely breath. I was weeping from my soul. I just wanted my life right. I needed grace and mercy.

Once I was done spilling my heart out, the judge continued. "I'm sentencing you to twelve months in a Federal Women's Prison with sixty months supervision upon release. I truly believe I will not see you in this courtroom again. But I'm giving you this time to think about what you want for your life."

Although I wanted to scream, Nooooo! I said, "Thank you. I

will do better and you will never see me in this courtroom again."

Surprisingly, she asked, "When would you like to turn yourself in? I know you have a newborn baby."

I was stunned. I had no idea I would have a choice!

"Umm, February, 2000," I said with apprehension. That would give me time to spend with my kids.

The Judge agreed and called Alisha to the stand. I was nervous for my twin sister. She was almost like an innocent bystander, she hadn't received one dime, so I was praying she just got probation.

When the judge said, "Alisha Readus, you are also sentenced to twelve months in a Federal Women's Prison," I could have fainted. Why was she getting the same time as me? I had two felonies and had actually gotten money. Alisha only had one felony. I didn't understand and I felt horrible for her.

Alisha sobbed loudly, which caused some of our family members to cry as well. I felt so guilty because I was such a bad influence on her. I cried for her, and felt sad for both of our kids. Our choices affected everyone around us, especially our children.

Things didn't get any better because Sam was sentenced to fifty-four months in prison and his anger was evident as he glared at us during his entire sentencing. Everything felt like an out-of-body experience. It didn't seem real, but it was happening right before my eyes.

Once court was over, I returned to my kids and Mark. He was pissed at me because of Sam, but at the same time, he felt bad for me.

"Asheera can just stay with me," he said after I'd spent all evening crying.

I was so lost, I didn't know what to do. Mark was a drug addicted alcoholic with very little patience. Did I want to leave my baby with him? And if I didn't, where would my kids go?

As I prepared to leave to go home, Mark began walking me to the stairs. I had the baby in her car seat, the baby bag, my purse, and was wearing high heels, and he didn't offer to carry a thing.

As I took the first step, my heel got snagged on the carpet, then Asheera and I went tumbling down the stairs headfirst. Everything I had in my hand went flying, including the baby's car seat with my baby in it. The seat flipped completely upside down as it rolled down the stairs.

Asheera's car seat was upside down when it landed on the hardwood floor. Mark's parents came running and he ran down the steps and turned Asheera's car seat upright. Asheera was crying and I could barely move, I was hurting all over.

"Is she okay?" I managed to say, despite the pain soaring through my body.

Mark examined her. "Yeah, she's just stunned, but she appears to be okay."

I wanted to take her to the hospital to be looked at just in case there were injuries that I didn't see. Mark agreed and his parents let us use their car.

Although I was in pain, nothing mattered more than Asheera being fine. On the way to the hospital, Mark kept blaming me for the fall. Although I wanted to curse him out, I began to wonder if I really was hurting my child, not just physically, but emotionally as well. That fall made me think of how damaging one mistake could be, one slip up in life and everything could be over. Just as me going to prison, that one choice changed the course of my life and the life of my children.

Thankfully, everything checked out fine with Asheera, and we were able to go back home that night. When I finally got Asheera settled, I laid in bed thinking about when would be the best time to begin serving my sentence.

I finally told myself the sooner I started, the sooner I finished, so I decided to go when Alisha turned herself in on October 25th, 1999. I could get started and then, I'd be finished and then I could return home and start my life over from scratch.

Chapter 36

Time was closing in and my life felt like it was coming to an end. I was so overwhelmed and had nothing to look forward to but prison time, so I decided to ask my mom could I come home until I had to leave to serve my sentence. I needed her. I needed stability for the rest of the time when I'd be out, and I needed peace and my mom's house was the only place where I could stay and get that until I left. My mom must have known I was heartbroken and on my last leg because she responded, "Yes," without hesitation.

Alisha and I began to me plans for our kids and that was a feeling that can never be explained. Fortunately, Shantel's grandmother was able to get her, and I talked to Mark's mother, and she decided that she would keep Asheera for me.

Shantel's grandmother lived in Huntsville, Alabama, so my mom drove my sister and I there. I was so lost for words during the entire drive. I needed to explain to my daughter what was happening. But what could I tell her? What would I say? 'Mommy's going to prison?' I was so sad and so ashamed.

I was still trying to formulate the right words when we pulled up to the house. We got out and I held my daughter's hand as we went in and sat for a while. But I couldn't delay it any longer and finally, it was time to go. I hugged her and told her, "Momma will be back. You're going to visit your grandma for a little while."

Shantel never before cried when I left her, but this time she did. It was like she knew I wouldn't be back for a while. I tried to hold back my tears as I walked out of the house. But once I got into the car, I burst into tears.

I cried the entire drive back. My heart was broken because she wouldn't understand what was happening. Sorrow filled my soul.

We made it back to Birmingham and it was time to drop off Asheera, who was now two months old. Although Mark's mother tried to reassure me that my baby would be okay, I was again so heartbroken because I knew she would not know me when I returned. She would be walking and have teeth when I finally came home. I would be a stranger in her eyes and that was the hardest thing to accept.

We made it back to our mom's house and sat with her for a while and then our father arrived. Our father would be driving us to surrender ourselves to prison in Florida. Alisha was going to Marianna and I was going to Coleman. They separated us because we looked too much alike and they considered us being twins a security risk.

When our dad arrived, we hugged our mom, I could once again, see the disappointment in both of their eyes. How could two stable parents have such messed up children? They both lived a life of respect. We never saw our father hit, curse, or shack up with a woman. We'd never seen our mom bring a man into the house. They were upright citizens with kids who were now convicted felons.

My sister and I got in the car with our dad and headed on the long journey from Alabama to Florida. I always enjoyed hanging with my dad and although he was disappointed, he never degraded us. He did sorrowfully say, "I never thought I would be driving you to prison. I always thought it would be to college."

That truth slapped me in the face, but my dad managed to do what he always did and that was make good conversation. We moved on from that subject and enjoyed talking the rest of the ride.

Alisha and I had never been separated for long periods of time, but now it would be a year or so until we would see each other again. That was an odd feeling because I truly was about to lose my best friend.

We dropped Alisha off and it felt like it did when I left my kids. My heart felt broken into a million little pieces.

My dad and I rode in silence to my prison. When we arrived, I was glad to see that at least it wasn't one of those dumps that I'd seen on TV. Still, everything still seemed unreal when I hugged and said goodbye to my dad and got out of the car with the $100 he gave me, my license, and social security card. Later, I realized that while he'd walked in with Alisha, he hadn't walked with me. I think he just couldn't endure the transition again.

I walked into the prison, gave them my name and the process began. It was very similar to when I got arrested, only this time, I also received my inmate number. That number would be the number that would take the place of my name. That number would be what I would now answer to.

They gave me brown scrub-looking clothes, with soft shoes that almost felt like socks. It was going to take a few days to get my official uniform. I got sheets, a pillow, and a blanket, then I proceeded to the Pod. The area was empty and the officer told me that most people were at work. When I entered the Pod, there was one lady there, cleaning.

"I'm Alma," she introduced herself to me, then started running off a list of do's and don'ts before even asking my name.

Alma helped me make my bed and gave me a run down on the daily process, including "count."

"They don't play with count around here," she said. "That's when you stand next to your cubicle and the officers come around and count the inmates. During this time, you can't talk because the numbers have to add up or they will have to re-count. If the number is still off, we go into lockdown."

I stood taking everything in as she continued talking.

"This your first stint?" she asked.

I nodded and she flashed a gentle smile.

"It'll get easier. Been here fifteen years myself."

I gasped. I couldn't even imagine how I was going to make one year. I'd die at fifteen.

Alma continued talking, showing me around. There was a shower, with doors, which I was grateful to see because I'd watched enough television to know you didn't see that often. There were also four TV rooms, with Spanish speaking stations, movies, video, and news only. There was also a washroom in the Pod as well.

After the grand tour, I headed to the nurse's station to have blood work done and get tested for HIV, Hepatitis B, and pregnancy. All of my tests came back negative and I was so very thankful considering the lifestyle I had led.

That night, I laid there in disbelief. I was on the top bunk staring at the ceiling, thinking of my life. I wanted to cry, but I didn't. Something just wouldn't let me cry anymore. I was determined to get my time over and get my life back. I felt so lonely without my kids, without being able to hear their voice, and the baby's cry. I missed smelling her and holding her little hand. I wondered how Shantel was feeling, and did she miss me already. I hoped she didn't because I didn't want her to feel sad. I just wanted my kids to be happy even if I wasn't there to bring them the happiness.

After the deep thoughts, I figured I should get some rest so I rolled over and tried to sleep. I don't think my roommate was too happy I was there because she fussed and said I moved too much, but she didn't say much else to me. She appeared to be a distant person, not the most friendliest, but I wasn't trying to make friends in prison anyway, especially not this sister!

The next morning I was prepared to move forward and find a job, since Alma had informed me that in this federal prison you had to work. She'd told me that I had my choice of where to work: kitchen, landscape, housekeeping, maintenance, production/plant, or working in a garage, fixing cars.

That was it. I wanted to fix cars. I wanted to learn something I didn't know so I applied for that and was fortunate enough to get the job. My pay was twelve cents an hour.

Of course, I knew that pay was ridiculous, but it was hammered home just how ridiculous the next morning when I had my first meeting with my counselor

". . . So I think that's about it," she said after she'd run down all the details with me. "But I do need to let you know that you have to start paying fines, fees, and restitution of $15,000."

I looked at her like she had lost her mind. How the hell was I going to pay that making twelve cents an hour? I was frustrated and upset because I didn't know what I was going to do. I could not do any more than what I could, so I just worked hard did my best.

Every day I went to work and ignored everyone around me. It was hard to relate to people when I was angry, hurt, and disappointed in myself. Before long, depression set in, and I ate for comfort. I ended up gaining forty pounds.

Part of my reason for sinking into a depression was because I rarely ever got letters. I never got a letter from one friend, not even Mark. My mom sent a few letters and money, and occasionally I would get a note from an aunt or a cousin. Once, my daughter's grandmother sent me a few pictures of my baby.

But Mark himself, he sent nothing - not one letter and not one dime. I felt all alone, and as far as I was concerned, out of sight, out of mind.

I never would have thought I could feel as empty as I did at that point in my life. Sometimes I would call people and once they heard it was me or heard the operator say it was "a collect call," they hung up.

So many nights I cried, "Why is no one here for me?"

The reality was that I messed my life up; my life had come to a complete stop and everyone else's life had kept going. I felt like I was stuck in time, repeating the same thing everyday: Wake up, get dressed, eat, go to work, and go to sleep. I had no freedom at all, but what did I expect. I'd lost my freedom to live or rather, I gave up my freedom when I committed the crime. I was the reason all of this happened. My choices led me to this place. I truly learned all I had was me!

One day, I was completely taken off guard when I was called into the counselor's office. I'd been in prison for months, and had no idea what she wanted.

When I got into the office, the counselor said to me, "Marisa, you need to pack your things. You're going on writ."

I frowned. "What's a writ?" I truly had no idea what that meant, and the only place I was interested in going was home.

"You are being subpoenaed to go back to court," she explained.

"Court? Court for what? They have all they need from me. I'm already in prison." I didn't want to go back to court. My mind started racing about all the other bad stuff I'd done. Had they found something else out and were going to prosecute me for that? Would that give me more time in prison?

"I don't know," she replied. "But you leave tomorrow morning, so be at the front at 6:30. You leave at seven."

I was baffled. I went to my little cubicle called a room, and gathered my things.

Samantha came in just as I was packing. "Hey, I heard them call your name. Is everything okay?" Samantha was a girl I worked with in the garage so I didn't mind her asking, and I'm actually glad she came in, because I was confused as hell.

"I'm not sure," I replied. "I'm going on writ tomorrow, but I have no idea why."

"Did you have a co-defendant?" Samantha asked.

"Yeah, but. . . I don't know," shaking my head as I placed the bag on the bunk.

"Well, I hope all goes well with you."

"Thanks."

As the news traveled, other inmates came to tell me what I could possibly expect.

"You may have to testify against someone, or you may have another case out there," one of them said.

Someone else said, "You may be gone for a while."

All of this advice and information wasn't making things better. Confusion ran through my head. I decided to send Alisha a letter letting her know that I was leaving, but telling her also that I would keep her updated.

The next morning, I cleaned out my area, got all my stuff and headed to the front office. There were shackles inside of a room, but I had no idea they were all for me. I went through a strip search, got handcuffed, and then, they put the shackles on my feet like I was some kind of stone-cold criminal. It was unreal! There were chains hanging from my hands that connected to my ankles.

The guards shuttled me out to a sixteen-passenger van out front. It was almost impossible for me to walk and I kept tripping. I had to take baby steps. I felt like a real animal with those chains on.

There was another person inside the van. A man. It was such a breath of fresh air to see the opposite sex. Although he and I could not talk to each other, it still was nice to have his eyes longingly run up and down my body.

We rode a couple of hours and finally we made it to the Tampa airport. As we drove up everything got surreal once again. There were men standing around a huge plane with big shot guns and wearing bullet proof vests. There were about ten other vans, obviously from other federal prisons. Each van was unloaded one at a time. We sat for forty-five minutes as we waited our turn. A lot of the prisoners stood in line and were patted down. They had to open their mouths, shake out their hair, and proceed to the plane. The stairs to get on the plane were even higher and harder than the ones on the van. One guy fell backward and tumbled down the stairs because it was just that difficult.

When my turn came, I mumbled and talked myself through it. "I can do this, I'm not going to fall," I muttered.

I made it up the steps and managed to get settled into a seat. The plane was filed with inmates, men on the left, women on the right. I had never flown before, so I was scared. On top of that, I was sitting by the window.

I sat there rethinking everything in my life as I stared at the man with the guns. Nothing was worth this horrible journey.

Finally, the engine roared and the jet rolled back. It moved faster and faster until we took flight. I still had nooooo idea where I was headed. It dawned on me at that moment that my life truly was not in my hands.

The plane landed and after a bit of time of getting out of the jet, getting into a van, then driving for a while, I found myself in a Georgia county jail. Right away I could see that this was a rough jail, definitely unlike the one I'd just left. About fifty of us were put into a holding cell with one bathroom and no door. The entire six hours I was there, I didn't use the bathroom. Other in-mates did, though, squatting like everyone wasn't staring at them.

There were so many different personalities, backgrounds, and crazies, that I was scared to even move. One lady had been carrying on a conversation with herself and thought, for whatever odd rea-son, that I wanted to join in. I sat there acting just as crazy, staring off and ignoring her as though she were invisible. Eventually, she moved on. I sat there listening in on other people's conversations. Most of them were local and had warrants or had gotten into some type of altercation.

Finally, after they fed us a sack lunch, they called several names. I sat, holding my breath until I heard, "Marisa Readus."

I jumped up, even though I still had no idea where I was going. My heart dropped when they simply took me to a booking room, booked me in, then took me to a cell. The cell was pretty big. It had two picnic tables in the middle and about five bunk beds on the right and another five bunk beds on the left. I was relieved to see there were only four girls in my cell. Less women, less drama. I found a bunk bed that was on the right, then I dragged my little mattress and made my bed as far away from everyone as possible. I laid down and closed my eyes.

After I'd been there for a couple of hours, someone muttered, "Is she sick?"

Still, I didn't open my eyes, I didn't move. I didn't want to. I was exhausted and sleeping allowed me to escape my reality. I laid there day dreaming, until I fell asleep.

The mind is a powerful place. I dreamed of being home with my kids, going to work, driving a car, going out to eat, and planning for vacations. I created the world that I wanted in my mind. I slept for twenty hours.

Days and days went by and I begged someone, anyone to tell me where I was going and why I'd been moved. But I got the same answer from everyone, "I don't know."

After a week, I was finally told that it was time for me to go. I was heading to Oklahoma.

"Oklahoma? For what?" I asked. It was nearing the holidays and Christmas was rolling around. I was going to spend my Christmas at a federal facility in Oklahoma where I didn't know a soul.

"Don't know," the guard mumbled, motioning for me to hurry up.

When the plane landed, it was cold and snowing. There were quite a few of us getting booked in. We were lined up and each one of us had a little room that reminded me of a dressing room. Of course, there were no doors. We stepped into our own area, undressed, then bent over and coughed, before changing into our clothes. That was so frustrating. Who wants a stranger eyeballing their private parts? It was never-ending embarrassment that never got easy.

Finally, they took us up to our rooms. This place was different than the other places. Here, I only had one roommate, who looked like she wouldn't hurt a fly, or skip a class. Honestly she looked like a stay at home mom, but what was she doing in prison? To fulfill my curiosity I asked the standard prison questions.

"What's your name?"

"Becky. Yours?"

"Marisa."

"What did you do to land here?" I asked.

Her big doe eyes were filled with sadness as she said, "I took the fall on a big case. I didn't do it, but I didn't want to be a snitch, so they gave me twenty-five years," she said." I really felt bad for her because she told me that she had a five-month-old baby and my baby was now four months old. I could feel her pain, but I also felt a sigh of relief because I knew I would be reuniting with my little one within the year, but she was stuck without her child for twenty-five years. I thought back on my crime, and although I didn't initially want to help the police, it wasn't because of some 'no snitching' rule. I just didn't want drama with Mark getting mad over me selling out his brother. Ultimately, I told whatever I needed to tell to get my sentence reduced.

But this woman was willing to do twenty-five years – away from her baby – for a crime she didn't commit just because she didn't want to snitch?

Over the next few days, I began to think that Becky's guilt and stress over her situation, drove her crazy because she talked to herself all the time. Every day and all day. Sometimes, she would talk while I was trying to sleep. Other than the excessive talking, Becky was not a bother.

I was happy to learn that they had a smoking section in this facility. I had been having nicotine fits that were making me miserable. Some people don't understand that smoking cravings are like sweet cravings, but they happen more frequently. Smoking is a true addiction. I must admit had I known it would be so hard to quit, I would have never started. But I needed the cigarettes more than ever because it had been a while since I'd been moved to Oklahoma – and I still had no idea why.

Chapter 37

One day a girl came into my room and showed me something interesting outside, just beyond the window break. There were several male inmates on the other side, standing in the window, doing all that they could imagine to entertain us.

After a few minutes of watching, the girl lifted her shirt and flashed the men.

"Girl, what the hell are you doing?" I asked her.

"Just having fun. Look, they love it," she giggled.

They definitely were into it. I didn't participate, but I did admire some of their bodies and laughed at how they were falling all out over her.

From that moment on, I put up a sheet to change my clothes because it just felt weird that I was being watched while getting dressed.

One day while sitting in the lounge area, a lady came up to me and said, "Hey, Alisha."

I was surprised to hear my sister's name, but I said, "Oh, I'm not Alisha. But hi."

"Wow, you look just like this chick named Alisha. Like the spitting image," she said in amazement as she stared at me.

I finally smiled. "She's my twin."

The woman relaxed like she was thankful she wasn't going crazy. "Oh wow. Really? I mean, of course, because y'all look just alike. Man, I thought you were her. I was locked up with her in Marianna."

"Oh. Yeah they separated us, they claimed we were a security risk since we looked so much alike.

"Well, make sure when you see your sister again you tell her Deja from Orlando said hi."

"Okay, I will." I saw her a few more times while I was there but we didn't talk a lot, she had her own group of girls that she was hanging with and I figured the less people I dealt with, the less drama I would have to contend with.

Christmas came and went, then I was once again, told that I was going to leave. I found out that I was going to Birmingham. The reason why was still unknown, but this time, just knowing where

I was headed took the edge off of my anxiety.

Once again I had to go back to the Atlanta county jail. I did not understand their route schedule because it made no sense. But I guess everyone had to go through Atlanta.

Fortunately this time, I was only there for a few hours and then the Marshalls arrived in a van to drive me to Alabama. This time I was taking a journey with a man, and although he wasn't necessarily my type he wasn't all ugly either. Although normal protocol stated that inmates couldn't talk to each other, the U.S. Marshalls we had were more laid back and he and I talked the entire time.

When we pulled up to the gas station they asked me what I wanted.

Looking out the window, I saw the McDonald's next door. "Can I have a hamburger from there?" I asked.

"Sure," one of the Marshalls said. "Just let us fill up and we'll head over there."

I was so happy. I know it was only a McDonald's, but you truly never know what you have until it is gone. Losing my freedom most definitely made me appreciate the little things in life.

I ordered a Big Mac meal and got chocolate chip cookies. I enjoyed every bite. Maybe it was because it had been so long, but that was the best meal I'd ever eaten. I didn't know how to act. Or maybe it was the fact that someone gave me what I wanted. Either way, I was beyond thrilled.

After the long drive from Atlanta to Birmingham, we arrived at the county jail. This was different from the city jail I'd gone to last time. When I arrived, I was booked in and taken to a cell that had two bunk beds and three other women. One woman had cuts on her arms and she said she was attacked by a baby tiger. I side-eyed her and kept it moving.

My other roommate was an awkwardly quiet and reserved girl that refused to talk or tell anyone why she was there. The third girl though, had me ready to get out of the cell asap.

"You heard about the case where that woman's two-year-old daughter was missing and they later found the baby chopped up inside of a closest?" the tiger lady asked.

"Oh, yeah. I remember seeing that on the news," I replied.

"That's her."

My mouth dropped open as the woman stared at me. "I was on crack," she said, like she really needed to explain to me. "I was on the stuff really bad, so I was out of my mind when I left my baby at a crack house to go to another crack house. When I got back, my baby was gone. I looked everywhere, but couldn't find her. I was pregnant with my second child, but they arrested me for neglect and abandonment and when my baby was born, the state took him."

"Yeah, whatever, you probably chopped your baby up yourself," Tiger Lady said.

"Screw you!" the woman yelled. "You don't know nothing about me!"

I put my hand on her arm to calm her down. "It's okay. I understand."

She seemed relieved that I said that. I didn't know why since she didn't know me from the next chick. The woman continued talking, telling me about how her daughter's death didn't seem real to her because she never saw her daughter again after that day and she never went to the funeral.

"They did find the man that took my baby," she said, glaring at

Tiger Lady. "Funny thing is, he's upstairs in the same jail. I want to be mad at him, I want to hate him, but I can't. It was all my fault."

My heart sank into such a deep sadness for the kids, but I respected her truth and her ability to take responsibility for her actions.

That night (and the nights that followed), she talked in her sleep, calling out her daughter's name, telling her, "Sweetie, get back up on the porch."

This woman was trapped and tortured in her mind. Listening to her in her sleep never got easy because I could never imagine that guilt or pain.

Every day at the county jail we were locked out of our room, and put into this huge room with all of the other inmates where everyone watched TV. The showers were also located in that area and they were so small you could barely move your arms, and the women didn't care, they would come out butt naked drying off, and flirting with other women in the process. I often sat in a corner at the top of the stairs until it was time to eat. One day when I switched gears and decided to watch TV some chick came over and sat by me, I glanced over at her and then back at the TV. She started talking "Hey what's your name?" she asked "hey I'm Marisa" I responded "oh ok nice to meet you" she said. She started talking some more "you know you look beautiful" all I could think is, this is some bullshit, lady I don't even get down like that, but I replied with a very dry "thanks." "They call me the black widow because women get caught up in my web." I laughed "you don't have to worry about me I'm good," as I stood up and walked away. I didn't know there was something in the air, but later that night another woman came up to me when we were heading to lock down. She sorta ran up on me all friendly and shit "hey what's your name, you look familiar?" She didn't look nowhere close to anybody I knew but I entertained her anyway "I'm Marisa, I have a twin maybe you know her" "naw ma, but ummmmm are you gay?" as she looked me up and down. I guess it was my French braids or something that had me looking boyish but I looked at her and said "naw I don't get down like that, but nice to meet you." I said, as I headed upstairs to my cell.

Two days after my arrival, I was called and told I was going to court, but I still didn't know why. Once again, I was shackled up and placed in a police vehicle. I rode toward the courthouse in downtown Birmingham, thinking of how close I was to home. I wanted desperately to just stop at the next light, get out and go back to my pre-crime life.

We passed a building that looked familiar. It was the Federal building where I was sentenced. We drove into an underground entrance and I was taken inside to a holding cell. What was I doing back here?

Chapter 38

Within an hour of returning to the Federal building, I was taken into a gray room that had nothing but a table and two chairs. The door swung open, and two of the Secret Service agents that I'd met the day we were caught, walked in.

I'm sure I looked super confused as one sat down across from me and the other stood behind him.

"Good to see you again, Marisa," the one sitting said.

I gave him a 'Really?' look and he continued.

"I'm sure you're wondering what's going on."

"That's the understatement of the year," I replied.

He twiddled his thumbs, taking his time, before he said, "Well, your girl isn't quite the friend you thought she was."

"What are you talking about?" I asked, getting frustrated with the constant runaround.

"Your partner in crime, Tamiko, is talking to anyone that will listen. She's placing all the blame on you."

That made me sit straight up in my chair. "What? That's a lie!"

Luckily, the agent nodded. "We think so, too."

The one standing chimed in, "We noticed the expression on your face when you learned there was no middle man and that she'd basically hustled you out of several thousand dollars claiming that there was."

I gritted my teeth and fell back in my seat. Yeah, I would never get over that but I guess the saying was true, there was no honor among thieves.

The agents filled me in on all the stuff Tamiko had been saying and by the time they were finished, I was pissed, betrayed, and willing to testify against Tamiko.

"Tamiko told us that Marisa is the one that came to me with this, to my understanding she was the one who stole the checks," one of the agents said.

Hold the hell up who stole what checks? I thought to myself.

I had no idea that any checks were stolen, but the agents told me that the checks were stolen from a fireman that worked in a nearby city. They also told me that Tamiko said in a sworn statement "Marisa was buying all kind of stuff with her money. She seemed to be in love with stealing from others."

I couldn't figure out if she really did say all of this, or were they just trying to get me to testify. I sat there and thought to myself, *Tamiko pled not guilty, which means she expects someone to take the fall for her indiscretion. She is in the middle of a trial because she has convinced herself that you are the one who came up with all of this, and now she is trying to convince the entire jury, so where does that leave you?"*

After thinking to myself I knew I was doing the right thing.

I was taken into the courtroom in handcuffs and there she was, sitting at the table. The woman I thought was my friend. She didn't even look at me.

It looked like court was already in session and I was led straight to the stand. They swore me in, then asked me a series of questions, many of them about people I didn't know. I answered each question as honestly as I could, but the prosecutor pushed, seeming to believe that I knew more when I honestly didn't. I was just as stumped as he was.

Eventually, he gave up and I was released. Now, I knew the full reason for my return to Birmingham. I didn't know that they'd caught Tamiko, and I didn't know what kind of charges she faced. She probably had a whole other organized crime scam going that I knew nothing about.

The ordeal was exhausting to say the least, but I was glad it was over. I returned to the county jail and the next day I was flown back to Oklahoma, where I would spend the new millennium.

I had planned to spend New Year's in bed, but the journey across the country and back had given me a lot of time to think. It was not only a new decade, but a whole new century. What better time to implement the new me.

So, although I didn't plan to be, I was awake and up when the clock struck midnight and everyone started shouting, "Happy New Year!" I joined in. I made a promise – not a resolution – that this year, my life would be better, my world would be better, and my choices would be better. I made a life changing decision on January 1, 2000. I chose to live, never allowing my past to dictate my future. I knew I could move past this point in my life. It was my choice!

On my way back to Florida we made a quick two day stop in Oklahoma, and then in Atlanta. While I was in Atlanta my room-mates were ratchet as hell. I tried so hard to just be peaceful and stay to myself, but one morning all hell broke loose. It was 5:00a.m. and whoever had to sweep and mop had to complete their task between 5:00 and 6:00a.m. Everyone in the pod was asleep except for two women who conveniently had been messing with the same guy on the outside.

One girl said, "Bitch, don't bring yo stank ass over here."

The other girl replied, "Who you think you talking to? I will kick your ass!"

"Well, if you feeling froggy, then jump, bitch"

I heard knocking sounds all over the place so I jumped out of bed. One of the girls mumbled, "If they don't cut this shit out they are going to get us all pepper sprayed, they don't break up no fights around here, they spray everybody!"

These girls were still going hard so I decided to break it up and grab the big girl, but the little girl was fast and ran up on the big girl.

"Y'all cut this shit out before we get pepper sprayed in this bitch and then I'm gone kick someone's ass up in here" I said, just as another girl ran up and grabbed the smaller girl. Somehow she got loose again and ran up to the big one but this time I grabbed the little one and slung her, and slammed the big girl on the bed. Finally somebody took the little girl to the other side of the pod. I held down the big girl and said "Hey, calm the fuck down! What the hell are you doing?"

"Man, fuck that bitch!" she said, as she sat up.

"Look, this ain't gon' work. You got to calm down or whatever you in here for is going to get a whole lot worse. Pull yourself together."

She listened, and then the guards came and took the smaller girl out and put her in another pod.

The next day I left, and boy was I ever so happy to make it back to prison.

Chapter 39

My attitude shifted that New Year's Day and the change was instantly noticeable when I returned to Coleman, Florida to finish my time. In fact, one afternoon, a former attorney who was serving time for tax evasion, approached me.

"You know, I really like your spirit," she said.

"Thank you," I replied.

She glanced around to make sure no one was listening. "So, let me share a little secret. I don't like to tell many people because you don't want everyone doing it."

At first, I thought she was about to tell me some gossip, which I really wasn't interested in. But the seriousness of her tone made me stop and listen.

"There's a little trick that could knock off some of your time," she whispered.

"What?" Now, she had my attention.

"Yeah, all you have to do is send a request to the judge and ask for an extra day."

"Why in the world would I ask for an extra day?"

"Because federal time is day for day. If you get a year, they'll make you serve a year, but if you get a year and a day, they're allowed to knock some time off for good behavior."

That made absolutely no sense to me, but I was willing to try anything to get out of jail. I still had to go to a halfway house upon my release – that was part of my sentence – but if the judge approved my request, I could go to the halfway house in eight months instead of ten months. I had nothing to lose and the lady was willing to help me write my request.

That same night I wrote a letter to Alisha advising her to do the same. God granted us both favor and within a week, our request was received, and accepted. Our sentence had changed! Our date for departure had changed. As I sit and think back on the favor we received, I can't explain why or how things had shifted in our favor. Maybe God knew both of our hearts, maybe He decided to be graceful, because we had been faithful. Faith worked for the both of us. The funniest thing is that neither one of us thought we would actually get it, sometimes it takes a little faith to make a drastic change occur in your life.

My attitude continued to improve, especially with the latest good news. While I waited for my release, I continued to work on cars and learn as much as I could.

One day in the garage, I was rotating tires on a 16-passenger van when my foot got stuck as I carried the front tire to the back. Suddenly, I lost my balance and tripped; there was a rail there, and my hand got wedged between the tire and rail. I dropped the tire and screamed. My hand was crushed and throbbing with pain. I felt every heartbeat in my hand.

The manager ran over. "Are you okay?"

"No!" I cried. "Oh, God it hurts so bad! Please don't touch it!" I shouted when he tried to examine it.

I could barely catch my breath, the pain was unreal. They took me to the nurse's station and everyone was convinced my hand was broken. We wouldn't know for sure until an X-ray was taken. Unfortunately, I didn't get an X-ray until a week later. I was so upset because I needed to do my review to go to the halfway house to work. They had to see if my behavior had been good, if my fees were paid, and if I was physically able to work. If I couldn't use my hand, I couldn't work, which meant I couldn't go home.

They wrapped my hand in a sling and I was taken off work for a while, so I kept myself busy by reading, watching Christian videos in the library, and going to church. I tried to work out, but the pain would stop me from exerting too much energy.

Although my hand still ached a week later, I went back to work. As soon as I arrived at work, the counselor called me into her office.

"Your work release has been confirmed," she said.

I was so excited I could have jumped out of my skin. I would soon see my kids, hug my kids, laugh with my kids! I could start my life back again.

I ran to the phone and called my mom.

"Great news, Mom," I said as soon as she answered. "I'm getting out!"

Silence momentarily filled the phone, then she said, "What?"

I proceeded to explain how I'd been approved for work release and would be going to a halfway house. After shedding tears and praise, she listened as I asked her to send me some clothes to wear home.

I felt like the dead had arisen when I asked for those clothes. I was going to be out in the real world, in real clothes. Words could never express that feeling.

Shortly after I got my good news, my sister also received a great blessing - my nephew. She sent me pictures and I could not wait to meet him. I was so inspired and encouraged that my family would soon be together again. I would have an opportunity to get it right this time. I actually had a second chance at life.

One day while I was at work vacuuming out a car Roxie thought she wanted to have some play time. Roxie is a Caucasian woman I use to work with, she was always on some other shit. She talked a lot, and always flirted with the guards. That day she took it a little too far with me and slapped me on my ass while I was bent over. Before I knew it I jumped up and grabbed her by her throat and threw her on top of the hood of the car. "Bitch what the fuck do you think you're doing?" I said angrily.

In shock she replied "I'm sorry I'm sorry!!"

"Don't you ever put your fucking hands on me I will kick your fucking ass!!" I slung her off the car. She continued to try to explain, but I cut her off "get the fuck out of my damn face before you get me put on lock down you dumb bitch!!" In the distance I saw the guard peeking over at me, and I looked at him and started to put the vacuum up. If I could just go a few more weeks without catching another case I would be good. Nobody was worth my time or my life and this little altercation surely could have been one to send me in the opposite direction of where I was trying to go.

A little more time passed on and the day came and it was time for me to go home. My clothes were waiting in the front office in the out take area. The pants and top my mother had mailed to me to wear were a little big because I managed to lose the forty pounds that I had gained, but I didn't care. I was just happy to be out of the prison uniform and heading home. I imagined myself throwing that uniform on the ground and setting it on fire, but since I didn't want to catch another case, I just politely handed it to the guard on my way out.

The counselor had already explained that I had an allotted amount of time to arrive to the halfway house. She'd stressed the importance of time management. Some inmates had been caught going to hotels, or trying to run off.

"You don't want to ruin this opportunity by doing something dumb," she warned me.

She didn't have to worry about that. I wasn't going to do anything that would send me back to prison. My only focus was getting to the halfway house. I had no time for games, playtime was over.

With the hundred dollars in my pocket that the counselor had given me and my bus ticket, I said my goodbyes, then headed out to the car. It felt freeing not to have any handcuffs, no shackles, just my ID and Social Security card, as well as a glimpse of freedom.

I was so happy and excited as I rode the bus back to Birmingham. I checked out the scenery like a child who had never been to a fireworks show; I was in awe of everything I saw.

During the journey home, those nine hours seemed like only

one. It gave me time to reflect where I had been, where I was going, and what I had to look forward to.

We had a small layover in a small town that I had never heard of and I got a little snack – and smiled when I realized that I was using my own money. The small things really do matter, and that Snickers and Mountain Dew tasted like Filet Mignon and Dom Perignon.

As I sat in that bus station, it also dawned on me that no one knew that I had just gotten out of prison. I looked like an everyday woman just going on a bus ride.

I arrived home later that night to see my mom standing there at the bus station, waiting for me and like a big kid, I ran to her and hugged her. I was happy to see her and just thankful that she came to get me. It was dark, so we got in the car and talked as she drove me to the halfway house.

The building stood out because it was green and sat right in the middle of an impoverished community. There was a picnic table in the back and big bright lights around the building. Although I had been to that side of town, and I'd seen the building before, I never knew it was a half-way house.

When we arrived, I grabbed the bag my mom brought for me. I didn't have much, but the little I had I was thankful for. When I went into the building, there were two people sitting inside of a bullet proof glass. I handed them my ID, then glanced around as they proceeded to tell me the rules.

"It's very important that you get and keep a job," the center director said, putting emphasis on the word keep.

"Yes, ma'am," I replied, my confidence at 110 percent. I was determined, and convicted felon or not, I was going to get a job.

After signing all of my papers, they showed me to the room I would stay in for the next three months. There were three bunk beds and seven regular twin beds. Everyone was asleep, so I quietly put my things away. As I was getting settled in, I noticed that there was one toilet with no door and two showers with curtains.

"Ewww," I mumbled, taking in the rest of the room. There was a huge mirror and four sinks. The light in the bathroom was on, so there was a light beaming into the sleeping area.

Even though I wasn't impressed by my surroundings, I finally laid down with a huge Kool-Aid smile on my face. It was time to move forward.

Chapter 40

The next morning I woke up excited and ready for the day to begin. I got dressed and headed out into the lobby area. I was not prepared for what I saw. Men, yes men, were everywhere.

I gazed around the room and noticed that most of them were buff. I thought to myself, *Stay focused, Marisa, stay focused.* That was hard because the temptation was everywhere.

I made it to the desk to get my two-hour pass to go out to Pizza Hut with my mom. It was wonderful to be out, and to be free. While riding with my mom, I told her about all the rules, and how I planned on getting a job.

"I'm confident that you can do it, Sweetie," my mother told me. She was a business teacher and had taught me very well, so she knew that I knew how to rock an interview.

My time with my mother was nice. I told her about my plans to get my life back together. I explained to her how much this is now my second chance on life to get it right. I don't know if she initially believed me but I do know that she knew I was a very focused, fearless person and was strong in character. Honestly I was just happy to be sitting with her, because I missed her. All I wanted to do was make things right with her.

During our conversation I asked her if I could come home one the weekends and she politely said no. I was surprised, hurt, but I also understood that I burned my bridges with her so I sucked up my pride and said okay. I never asked again, nor did I ask her for much else because I didn't want to be a burden. I was just thankful for that moment we had, and for what she had already done. I was also thankful for that pizza. I enjoyed every cheesy bite like it was a thousand dollars a plate.

When I was in prison, my cousin told me she knew a guy who could help me get a job. The man worked for a utility company and was in a very high position, so I'd kept his number and called him. He wanted to meet me and we made arrangements for him to come by the halfway house the next day to interview and to get my resume.

Before I'd left the prison, I'd updated my resume so I was prepared when he arrived. I was wearing a two piece suit and my hair was done, pulled back in a bun, thanks to my mom taking me to the beauty supply store.

The counselors were very impressed with my appearance.

"I've never seen an inmate look so nice for an interview," one of them told me.

"Thank you," I confidently replied.

Fifteen minutes later, I was standing in front of the man, who was six feet tall with brown skin, and was dressed in a business suit. He appeared to be nice, and concerned about helping me.

"I really want to see you get back on your feet," he told me. "We don't have any jobs open in the offices, but I can find you something at a construction site."

That didn't matter to me. I was happy because I needed to work and was no stranger to labor, so I was ready.

A few days later, I met the site manager and was hired to help install heating and cooling units in corporate buildings. Unfortunately, I didn't have any work clothes, or steel toe boots but my cousin's friend told me he would get me what I needed. I was thankful he really wanted to help me. True to what he'd told me, the next day he showed up and drove me to the store where he bought me a few work clothes and boots. Afterwards, he took me to get something to eat.

When we got back to the halfway house, I told him, "Thank you sooooo much. I truly appreciate it."

Before I could open up the door to get out of the car, he leaned over to kiss me. But, I pushed him away. "No! What are you doing?" I screamed.

"I thought you appreciated everything I've done." He had the nerve to look confused.

"I do, but you're married," I replied, something he'd told me during the first meeting we had.

"So?" He frowned. "I thought you wanted. . . " He fell back against the car seat. "Never mind."

He didn't understand; I didn't want that old life. I didn't want married men anymore. I wanted to be a better person. After that day, I never saw him again.

The weekend finally rolled around and I was proud of myself because I accomplished getting a job my first week out. Now it was time to see my kids!

My mom and my sister brought my girls to see me and I was so nervous, but excited I could barely contain myself. I wondered if my little baby, Asheera, would remember me or like me, and would Shantel ask me questions I wasn't ready to answer yet.

When I saw them, I hugged them and tears came to my eyes. I missed them so much, words couldn't express.

Although Asheera didn't know who I was, I knew in my heart that she would grow to love me as her mother - the woman who gave birth to her and loved her more than life itself. Just like I knew before I went to prison, Asheera was already walking and she had teeth. She babbled a lot of unknown words that sounded like music to me as I sat and smiled.

Shantel was so happy to see me. We talked and she told me all about her visit with her grandma. I told her that I was going to get an apartment so she and her sister could have their own room together. We were all so happy.

Although I didn't see Shantel anymore until after I got out of the halfway house, I was fortunate to see Asheera two more times during my three months stay. I didn't understand why people wouldn't bring my kids to see me more often, and what was even worse, is that I didn't understand why Mark never brought Asheera or came to visit himself.

But this time, I refused to wallow in a pity party. I just focused on the end – getting out for good and getting my kids.

Chapter 41

Unfortunately, I began to get sick while I was working in construction because my body could not handle the manual labor. It was time to change jobs, and a girl told me about a plant that made plastic products that was hiring, so I decided to call and find out how I could get a job there. They told me to come in and I tried like crazy to get someone to take me to the plant, but unfortunately I had to ride the city bus.

The only problem was, the bus dropped me off two miles away from the actual plant. I calculated the time in my head. It was tight and I wouldn't make it back in time to the halfway house if I walked.

Although I was afraid of being late, I decided to go for it. The drop off location was at the top of a very high hill, and there was nothing but trees and woods on both sides of me. I heard a noise in the bushes, and I took off running like a mad woman down that hill. I turned those corners left and then right, and then left again. I was not going to stop until I saw light.

Finally, I made it to the bottom of the hill and there was a gas station there. I was hot, sweaty, and sad. I began to cry as I sat at a table. Then, I heard a voice say, "Hey, are you okay?"

I looked up at the young, white woman. "No," I admitted as I wiped the sweat and tears away. I don't know why, but I just started talking. I told her about everything because at that point I had absolutely nothing to lose.

When I was finished, she smiled warmly, then said, "I can give you a ride."

I jumped up because I wasn't expecting that. "Thank you! Thank you so much."

She drove me to the job site and I smiled with gratitude when she pulled up to the front door.

"Thank you, again. I'm so sorry I don't have but a few dollars for gas."

"No, don't worry about it. Good luck."

"Thanks."

I went in and after a short interview, I got the job on the spot. When I walked out of the building, the woman was still sitting there in her car, waiting for me.

"I'll take you back to the halfway house so you'll make it in time," she said.

I couldn't help it. I started to cry. God had sent me an angel. And I could only pray that was a sign of things to come.

As my time wore down in the halfway house, I continued to work, and I did everything that I could to stay away from the men. That is, until I met Calvin.

Calvin was everything I wanted in a man – fine, handsome, a beautiful smile, and a great personality. He helped me pass time because of his positive outlook on life.

Calvin and I were around each other every day and had a lot of good conversations. We were attracted to each other, but attraction equals distraction, which I did not need at that time in my life.

One Friday night when I was off work, and so was he. There was an irresponsible guard on duty who let us all do whatever we wanted and Calvin and I did exactly that. I think we both had been without the touch of another man or woman for so long, that we just craved the intimacy. We didn't think about how awkward it would be afterward since we lived in the same house every day. The rules stated that we were not to have relations with other inmates, male or female. I honestly don't know how they expect for men and women who've been in prison without sex to act civilized around each other, but that was the rules.

Things eventually got uncomfortable because my expectations went to places they should not have gone. I didn't want to be his hoe, but neither did I need a relationship either. He had nothing to offer me and I had nothing to offer him. We both were trying to get our lives back together.

A few weeks after Calvin and I were together, he went on a pass with some woman, and boy did that make me mad. But there was nothing I could do but be mad and feel stupid because he was truly not my man.

After that, I decided to keep my distance from him and stayed in the girls pod (an open room with no walls between the beds) and rest on my bunk, more often to avoid him. But one day, I heard him and some of his friends talking about me outside of my room. He was telling them how he'd "Hit that and now had me hooked."

That did it! I jumped up, stomped into the hallway, and went off.

Raising hell in jail was not the smartest move, because that would be the move that would get me moved right back to prison. But although I could have gotten into a lot of trouble behind that stunt, I didn't because my behavior had been on point the entire time I'd been there. I made a choice to stay focused and start looking for a place for my children and I to live. Drama was not what I needed, so Calvin had to be deleted from my attention and my life.

During my search for housing, I was fortunate to come upon an apartment at the YWCA that was recently renovated; so I applied. Within two weeks, I found out that I was approved, but only for the single women's unit because the family unit was full. After speaking to my daughters' grandmothers and explaining my situation, they were happy to let the girls stay with them a little longer so I could get on my feet.

The following week, it was time for me to leave the halfway

house and I moved into my own little apartment. It was a tiny space with a sitting area, kitchen, bedroom, and small bathroom. But it was mine, my own place to call home. My own address with my name on it. There was peace within those walls. No people, no officers, no one telling me when to come and when to go. I couldn't have asked for anything more.

A shelter donated sheets, pillows, and dishes to me, so I was all set.

What made things even better is my twin, and best friend was coming home and we both would be free and back together again. Things were shifting in our life, and we both were two determined women getting our life back together for us and our kids.

I remember standing at that bus station waiting with my mom, and Jonathan. I was so excited I couldn't wait to see her and meet my new nephew. She got off the bus and we were like little five year old girls playing outside again happy like to puppies. We couldn't stop smiling, it was also good to see Jonathan meet his new son, although I wondered what type of father he would be, I was really glad he was there. It was a beautiful day, and I was so happy!

Shortly after moving in, I decided to look for a job closer to where I lived so I could walk to work. God sure does answer prayers because I met a lady who worked at a plasma center and she told me they were hiring phlebotomists. Although I didn't have phlebotomy experience, I did have four years medical experience as a CNA and I decided to apply and once again, I got the job. I actually got the job while I was on crutches because I injured my leg at the plastic plant. I wasn't worried because the woman who hired me was actually very impressed with my determination for hopping all the way to the interview. Although I told her I was a convicted felon she didn't really seem to be phased by it, she was very welcoming and non-judgmental.

I worked twelve hour shifts, five days a week most of the time. Then, I started going to school to be a Medical Assistant and cut my hours back just a bit a couple of times a week. I was doing it.

Working, school, I was getting my life together.

In February 2001, I got my car - a Dodge Neon - and it felt like it was a Mercedes.

Now, I could visit my kids when I wanted, drive myself around when I wanted, see my probation officer when I needed to without having to walk miles to get to her. I was feeling like a million bucks.

I believe in advancing, so after seven months, I decided to get a better paying job; I applied for a lab position at a hospital. The hours sucked, but the pay was three dollars an hour more than what I was getting paid; so I took the position. At that point I was able to move out of the YWCA and get my own apartment: a two bedroom, one bath for $295 a month. My sister told me about a place where she got her furniture and I was able to get my entire house furnished with $100. And making things even better, my apartment was right around the corner from my twin sister.

After I was settled into my apartment, the greatest day of my life came. I got my kids back! I was so happy to watch them in our home. For so many nights after we all came there together, I would stand in their door and just watch them laying in their beds. My soul was filled with joy. And I would never again do anything stupid to take that joy away. I had truly broken through the bars, and the days I often dreamed of in prison, became a reality. My future was now and I wasn't going to miss it - nor ever mess it up again.

Message from Alisha...

To the readers: I would first like to say thank you so much for supporting my twin sister and I. This journey of *Breaking Through the Bars* has taught me that the only limits that were in my life were the limits that I placed there. I did not have to commit a crime in order to be successful, I did not have to settle for bad relationships, and I did not have to be a statistic. It was truly my life, and my choice.

Today, I wake up and I look around at my wonderful children and see what life is truly about. My wonderful seven children: Rashard, RaMon, Romel, Rasheed, Racheal, Roosevelt, and Reanna are the reasons why I have to keep going. They are a piece of all that I am and I want them to live with the better part of me in them.

I hope this book has given you a little insight on how powerful choices, and change, can be. As I sit and glance out of the window, I see a present time that makes my past worth it all. I am a better me, a better mother, and have a greater purpose because I did not stop, and I didn't give up on what I knew would be a better future my family. Thank you Jesus for another opportunity to get it right this time. I am thankful.

Alisha Readus and her seven children: Rashard (19), Ramon (17), Romel (15), Rasheed (13), Racheal (13), Roosevelt (9), and Reanna (9). You are not imagining things - there are two sets of twins in this powerful family!!

Message from Marisa...

I pray so much that this book was a blessing to you. My biggest desire is that you were inspired, and empowered. Going through as much as I have gone through taught me independence, gave me strength, and gave me wisdom.

Making a choice for change was not easy because so many people expect so much of you. I had to learn to live to be a better me and not regret letting the people go who hurt my life. What I gained from the tears that I shed many nights was that everything was truly going to be okay. I learned if I lived another day I had another opportunity to get it right. I had another opportunity to change.

Thank you to my kids, Shantel Ross, Asheera Horton, and Gabriel Ross have been my biggest support and motivation. My nieces and nephews whom I love so much, are also the fuel that keeps my engine going. Above all else, My Lord and Savior Jesus Christ, who has directed all of my steps throughout this journey.

Thank you to my readers for taking the time to share our story. You are so appreciated.

Marisa Readus and her daughters, Shantel Ross (20 years old) and Asheera Horton (16 years old). (Not pictured - Gabriel Ross, one-year-old).

A Family that plays together…

Stays together....

If You Liked

Breaking Through the Bars

you'll like…

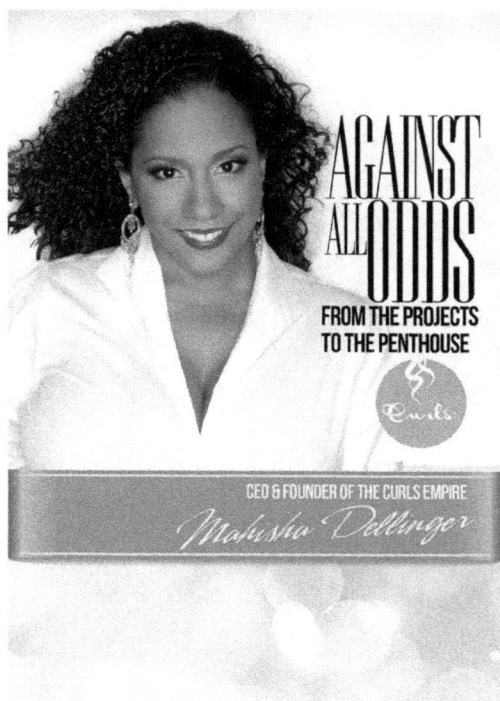

Turn the page for a Sneak Peek…

Introduction

I've always known I was destined for great things. Don't ask me how I knew. I just did. It definitely couldn't have been my environ-ment. After all, the mean streets of Sacramento can shatter any-one's dreams. In fact, my Meadowview neighborhood was dubbed "Danger Island" and although it was nestled between the affluent Pocket/Green haven area and lower middle class, Mack Road, it was not a place you wanted to be caught outside after dark.

I definitely didn't have the support at home. It's not that my family didn't believe in me and want more, but my mother was working so hard – and so long – that dreams (hers and mine) took a back seat.

However, I knew that I wouldn't allow someone else to write my story. I knew that my story was bigger than the impoverished streets I called home. And now, as my company, CURLS LLC, boasts its best year to date, I look back and reflect on where I've been and where I'm going.

I'm hoping that my story will inspire others to take their own journeys, to not let their pasts dictate their future, to go for their dreams and not let anything or anyone get in their way. While my story may be deemed a rags to riches tale, it's bigger than that. So much bigger. It's about an ordinary girl who decided she was capable of extraordinary things. It's about a woman who took all the obstacles tossed in her path of life and used them as step-ping-stones to bigger and better things.

I truly have come from humble beginnings and as I worked my way up through the rigors of corporate America, the ups and downs of being an entrepreneur, the frustrations of trying to maintain a proper work-family balance, I've learned some valuable lessons. They are lessons that I share with you in the coming pages. From the pitfalls to the pinnacles, I bare it all.

Now, as my company – which started from my kitchen – is poised to post-record sales, I'm sharing my journey. Not only of how I overcame an impoverished background to pursue my passion, but also of how I went from just dreaming to *doing*. With valuable, applicable tips, it is my hope that after reading, the entrepreneurial spirit within you will be awakened.

My story can be your story. And if you walk away with nothing else, I hope that you'll understand my motto: When you wake up in the morning you have two choices - go back to sleep and dream your dreams, or wake up and chase your dreams.

I choose the latter. What will your choice be?

Mahisha

Chapter 1

A Tale of Two Worlds

I'm not supposed to be here.

At least that's what the statistics said. According to all the studies, and the declarations of negative people in my life, if I did survive my gang-riddled neighborhood, it would be unwed with several children by my side, a dead-end, low-paying job, and a future that lacked hope. That's what the statistics said.

But I had a different ending for my story.

I never have settled for the norm. Even as a little girl, from a broken home, I knew that my destiny was greater than my existence. After all, I'd survived abuse, and my life had been spared more times than I could count.

Given my background, I could've easily become that sassy, tell-you-off, around-the-way girl who ran with the dope boys and held her own in the streets. Quite the contrary, though, I was about as close to perfection as you could get in a child.

With flopping pigtails and a smile that melted everyone I met, people in the neighborhood knew that I wasn't like the rest of the girls. From a very young age, I was a very self-motivated, independent, and simply, an easy child to raise. I never got in trouble (I would occasionally mouth off, but my mother was quick to pop me in my mouth to get me back in line). I was where I was supposed to be, when I was supposed to be there.

However, one day, I wasn't where I was supposed to be - at John Sloat Elementary School. To this day, I believe my mother's boyfriend, Willie, is to blame.

My daily routine was the same - my mom left for work at 7 a.m. I got myself up, dressed, and off to school by 8:30 a.m. Willie was always the last person to leave before me, he knew that the garage was my only way out. I didn't have a house key (my brother did because he always made it home from school before me, so I didn't need one). Willie knew that I exited through the kitchen into the garage, manually lifting the exterior garage door. This day was like no other, except when I went to lift the wooden garage door to head to school, it was locked. I had already locked the door to the house so I couldn't get out. I was stuck!

I knew I would miss school that day. I hated missing school. I hated getting behind. Still, I didn't panic, at first, even though I was afraid. I tried to pick the lock - no luck. I was eight years old and had no idea what I was doing. I tried to kick in the door. Nothing. I weighed all of sixty pounds so I don't know what I thought I was doing anyway. After accepting that I wasn't going anywhere, I had to find a way to keep busy, for nearly nine hours. I sorted and folded the clothes in the dryer. I swept the entire garage, organized every item I could get my hands on. When I finished that I discovered that only an hour had passed!

I reviewed my spelling words again, I checked my homework again, and I read another chapter in my history book. After three hours I started to panic. I was really scared and started to weep. My cries were interrupted by a voice.

"Hello, is there someone in there?"

It was the mailman!

"Yes! I'm locked in!" I screamed.

"What is your name?" he asked through the garage door.

"Mahisha. Mahisha Vernon," I anxiously replied. "Help me, please. I'm stuck in here."

"Who can I call for you?" he asked.

"Please call my mom," I said, giving him my work number.

"Okay, I'll be right back."

I would later learn that he went to my neighbor's house and

called my mother. She was frantic but she couldn't leave her job, so she called my uncle, Calvin, who lived close by. As long as I can remember, my Uncle Calvin always came to our rescue. When my mother's car was stolen, for the third and final time, a week before Christmas, he gave her a car to use for two years until she could get another one. He has always had a kind, giving spirit and that day was no exception. Uncle Calvin came to my rescue ten minutes later! He cut the lock off of the garage door, even cutting up his hand pretty badly. I don't think I'd ever been so happy to see someone! And I was even happier to be out of that garage. Uncle Calvin gave me a big hug and took me for a ride on his motorcycle. My mom was upset with Willie that day, even though he swore he didn't purposely lock the garage. I didn't believe him, but we could never prove otherwise.

As much as I wanted to go off, I let the incident go. That was my nature. I was far from a troublemaker. There were never any surprises me with so there was never any need to ground or punish me. Yes, my mother was able to relax with me. It was, however, a totally different story for my brother. He was more than a handful and caused my mother enough grief for the both of us.

My parents never married. They were from two different worlds and the worlds could never seem to mesh. While his family lived a life of privilege, my mother's family lived a life of poverty. So for her, and subsequently us, every day was a struggle. In those days, women didn't file for child support and so the burden of caring for me and my brother fell solely on my mother. Don't get me wrong, my dad took care of my living expenses, but my day-to-day existence was meager.

Every day I saw a tale of two worlds, from the impoverished school I attended, to the graffiti laden streets that I walked, I saw the worst that Sacramento had to offer. But just as soon as I settled into that life, I would be whisked away to spend weekends in the suburbs with my father. There, I would experience the best that life had to offer. Visits to museums, exotic restaurants, and cultural landmarks one day. Drive-bys, gang wars, and home invasions the next.

But my primary world was with my mother, where I fell asleep to the sound of gunfire, where it was nothing for a gang to come kick in your front door. In fact, I saw the gang life up close and personal as my brother was a member of the Meadowview Blood's, a notorious street gang.

As vastly different as the two worlds were, each played a role in the woman that I've become. As a little girl, those two worlds became the sum of my existence.

My parent's backgrounds were so different. My dad's family put an emphasis on education, all of their descendants ended up doing something amazing with their lives. My dad was an engineer and almost everyone in his family was educated. Eric Holder, who served as US Attorney General twice, married a cousin on my dad's side, Sharon Malone, who is an obstetrician and gynecologist. If you Google another relative, Vivian Malone, you'll see she did so many amazing things in history. She was the first black woman to graduate from the University of Alabama, amongst many other amazing accomplishments. Jeff Malone is a retired NBA star. Most of our relatives have completed college and all are doing well in life.

So maybe that drive to succeed is ingrained within me. All I know is for all that I did inherit from my father's side; I inherited just as much from my mother's side.

Living in the hood gave me the strength, endurance, perseverance, determination, and sheer will to fight. I am one tough cookie. Don't be fooled by my Chanel bag and Louboutin heels.

Sure, my mom's side of the family was the total opposite. My grandmother, the daughter of a slave, lived in the hood, had nine children, and adopted the tenth. Her mother raised her first two children. She was married and left by a host of husbands. Given all of her trials and tribulation, she led by example. She was a praying woman with faith so strong she didn't worry about where their next meal was going to come from.

Because of the time I spent with my dad, I started to feel like I didn't belong in the hood. My dad dressed me, he bought me expensive clothes that I wore in the hood with kids who wore the same clothes every day. I had the same amount of money they had — I was poor. I never felt like I belonged anywhere. I was an oddity.

So, while he was showering me with my material needs, my mother made sure all of my emotional needs were met.

I learned about the finer things in life with my dad. How I deserved nice things, how education and financial security could lay the foundation for a successful future.

From my mother, I learned the essence of hard work. As long as I can remember, my mom never was without a job. But that working took its toll on us. Mom was always gone early in the morning, so I remember from second grade on, I would get myself up on time, comb my hair, get myself dressed, prepare my breakfast, pack my snack and walk to school.

"There goes little Miss Vernon," my neighbor would say as I traipsed down the street. "Always on point."

I'd wave, never breaking my stride. I took pride in everyone knowing how I was always so responsible.

We moved every couple of years, so I changed schools a lot and had to learn to make friends fast, adapt quickly, and be outgoing. I spent second grade in one school, third grade in another school and so on and so forth each year.

While my schooling may not have been consistent, there was one thing that was constant. Church.

I spent a lot of time at church when I was growing up. My mom gave her life back to God when I was in the sixth grade. Our lives changed forever when we joined Zion Church in Jesus Christ, a strict Apostolic church that didn't allow women to wear pants, make up, or jewelry.

As much as I appreciated all I was getting from church, there was a time when I felt embarrassed because it got to the point that I was teased incessantly, for being the "weird church girl that only wore dresses." Add to that fact that I was in the seventh grade, flat-chested and shy, and it made for a miserable existence.

But little did I know, puberty was about to change my life.

Want more?

Get your copy
wherever books are sold...

www.BrownGirlsBooks.com

www.ingramcontent.com/pod-product-compliance
Lightning Source LLC
Chambersburg PA
CBHW032117040426
42449CB00005B/170